Teaching and Learning in the 21st Century

Advances in Innovation Education

Series Editor

Bharath Sriraman (*The University of Montana, USA*)

International Advisory Board

Don Ambrose (*Rider University, USA*)
Danah Henriksen (*Arizona State University, USA*)
Svanborg Rannveig Jónsdóttir (*University of Iceland*)
Marianna Papastephanou (*University of Cyprus*)
Andrew Penaluna (*University of Wales – Trinity Saint David, UK*)
Larisa Shavinina (*University of Quebec, Canada*)
Renu Singh (*Phoenix Union High School District, USA*)
Elizabeth Sumida Huaman (*University of Minnesota, USA*)
Ian Winchester (*University of Calgary, Canada*)

VOLUME 6

The titles published in this series are listed at *brill.com/aiie*

Teaching and Learning in the 21st Century

Embracing the Fourth Industrial Revolution

Edited by

Jayaluxmi Naidoo

BRILL
SENSE

LEIDEN | BOSTON

All chapters in this book have undergone peer review.

Library of Congress Cataloging-in-Publication Data

Names: Naidoo, Jayaluxmi, editor.
Title: Teaching and learning in the 21st century : embracing the fourth industrial revolution / edited by Jayaluxmi Naidoo.
Description: Leiden ; Boston : Brill Sense, [2021] | Series: Advances in innovation education, 2542-9183 ; volume 6 | Includes bibliographical references and index.
Identifiers: LCCN 2021015536 (print) | LCCN 2021015537 (ebook) | ISBN 9789004460379 (hardback) | ISBN 9789004460355 (paperback) | ISBN 9789004460386 (ebook)
Subjects: LCSH: Education--Effect of technological innovations on. | Educational technology. | Teaching--Methodology. | Education--Aims and objectives. | Industry 4.0.
Classification: LCC LB1028.3 .T3745 2021 (print) | LCC LB1028.3 (ebook) | DDC 371.33--dc23
LC record available at https://lccn.loc.gov/2021015536
LC ebook record available at https://lccn.loc.gov/2021015537

Typeface for the Latin, Greek, and Cyrillic scripts: "Brill". See and download: brill.com/brill-typeface.

ISSN 2542-9183
ISBN 978-90-04-46035-5 (paperback)
ISBN 978-90-04-46037-9 (hardback)
ISBN 978-90-04-46038-6 (e-book)

Copyright 2021 by Koninklijke Brill NV, Leiden, The Netherlands.
Koninklijke Brill NV incorporates the imprints Brill, Brill Hes & De Graaf, Brill Nijhoff, Brill Rodopi, Brill Sense, Hotei Publishing, mentis Verlag, Verlag Ferdinand Schöningh and Wilhelm Fink Verlag.
All rights reserved. No part of this publication may be reproduced, translated, stored in a retrieval system, or transmitted in any form or by any means, electronic, mechanical, photocopying, recording or otherwise, without prior written permission from the publisher. Requests for re-use and/or translations must be addressed to Koninklijke Brill NV via brill.com or copyright.com.

This book is printed on acid-free paper and produced in a sustainable manner.

Contents

Preface VII
Acknowledgments XII
List of Figures and Tables XIII
Notes on Contributors XIV

1 Exploring Teaching and Learning in the 21st Century 1
   Jayaluxmi Naidoo

PART 1
The 21st-Century Curriculum

2 The Fourth Industrial Revolution: Implications for School Mathematics 13
   Ajay Ramful and Sitti Maesuri Patahuddin

3 Embracing the Fourth Industrial Revolution by Developing a More Relevant Educational Spectrum: Coding, Robotics, and More 30
   Reginald Gerald Govender

PART 2
The 21st-Century Classroom Environment

4 Visualizing as a Means of Understanding in the Fourth Industrial Revolution Environment 53
   Vimolan Mudaly

5 Transforming the Classroom Context: Mathematics Teachers' Experiences of the Use of Technology-Enabled Pedagogy for Embracing the Fourth Industrial Revolution 71
   Jayaluxmi Naidoo

PART 3
The 21st-Century Teacher

6 Teaching and Assessment Skills Needed by 21st-Century Teachers: Embracing the Fourth Industrial Revolution 89
   Septimi Kitta and Jaquiline Amani

7   Pre-Service Technology Teachers' Learning Experiences of Teaching Methods for Integrating the Use of Technologies for the Fourth Industrial Revolution   106
    Asheena Singh-Pillay

8   Pre-Service Teacher Educators' Experiences of Using Mobile Technologies in the Teaching and Learning of Mathematics and Technology Education for the Fourth Industrial Revolution   119
    Asheena Singh-Pillay and Jayaluxmi Naidoo

PART 4
The 21st-Century Student

9   Teaching and Learning Science in the 21st Century: A Study of Critical Thinking of Learners and Associated Challenges   139
    Yashwantrao Ramma, Ajeevsing Bholoa, Shobha Jawaheer, Sandhya Gunness, Henri Tin Yan Li Kam Wah, Ajit Kumar Gopee and Deewarkarsingh Authelsingh

10 Genius-Hour: Student-Led Learning in the Fourth Industrial Revolution   157
    Jennifer M. Schneider and Guy Trainin

Glossary   173
Index   176

Preface

It is exciting to live in the 21st century amidst transformation and adaptation as we teach and learn in the era of the Fourth Industrial Revolution. It is also daunting as education is in the throes of immense transformation as we try to negotiate the 'new normal' for education within the ambits of the COVID-19 pandemic era. Through the use of technology-enabled pedagogy and online platforms, education is more available, to members of society, in more places, and more ways than ever in human history. And, maybe, for this reason, these are exciting and challenging times for education globally. This edited volume is a noteworthy contribution to understanding responses to one fundamental question: In the 21st century, what does it mean to teach and learn within the era of the Fourth Industrial Revolution? It uses the lens of the Fourth Industrial Revolution to look at what is happening globally within Basic and Tertiary Education.

All chapters within this edited volume probe responses to this critical question. Probing is done by engaging with issues about teaching and learning in the 21st century. For example, aspects of the curriculum, classroom environment, teachers and students are engaged with by authors in this edited volume.

Part 1 focusses on issues concerning the 21st-century curriculum; Part 2 concentrates on the 21st-century classroom environment, Part 3 focuses on teachers in the 21st century, and Part 4 concludes the edited volume by engaging with research and examples focussing on students in the 21st century.

The volume is bold in its scope and yet supported in its focus on actual global examples. It looks at various developments in teaching and learning but does so by focusing on international case studies and examples. Most importantly, it is essentially universal in its position. This global viewpoint, in itself, is an important inspiration. This is not a book of expectations about the future of education as much as it is a guide to traversing the many strengths and challenges we experience as we teach and learn within the Fourth Industrial Revolution. Through emphasizing experiences from around the world, it points the reader in the direction of good practice. The importance of adopting an interdisciplinary approach is emphasized throughout, as teachers and students strive to embrace the challenges and strengths of teaching and learning within the 21st century with imagination, determination and interest.

In this universal community of practice, we can all learn from each other. The case studies and samples of good practice in this volume offer notable examples of how educationalists from around the world are working within their educational contexts to transform their educational environments to embrace the Fourth Industrial Revolution. The educational contexts of the Fourth Industrial Revolution and the challenges and strengths of education are essential underpinnings for this discussion. The case studies in this edited volume look at the question of teaching and learning within the 21st century from numerous viewpoints. Still, all are grounded in the notion of embracing the Fourth Industrial Revolution. In culminating the global thoughts and practices, this book makes a noteworthy contribution not only to our understanding of what it means to teach and learn within the 21st century but also to signal practical steps that readers could take. These practical steps can influence the transformations that will occur as we embrace the Fourth Industrial Revolution as we teach and learn in the 21st century.

Chapters within this edited volume exemplify authentic case studies situated within diverse global contexts. Authors have provided discussions and case studies focusing on the 21st-century curriculum, classroom, teacher and student. Also, responsive and innovative pedagogies for the 21st-century classroom are revealed and explored. Thus, this volume draws attention to global case studies and examples of good practice focusing on 21st-century teaching and learning in the domains of the Fourth Industrial Revolution. The findings of these various researchers within global contexts exhibit that teaching and learning ought to transform to embrace the Fourth Industrial Revolution successfully. Globally, these findings have relevance when considering the role of the Fourth Industrial Revolution within educational contexts.

Chapter 1 explains the notions of the Fourth Industrial Revolution and explores issues of teaching and learning in the 21st century. Aspects about the 21st-century curriculum; the 21st-century classroom environment; teachers in the 21st century, and students in the 21st century are introduced in this chapter.

Thereafter, the volume proceeds with nine chapters. Part 1 encompasses two chapters that address issues concerning the 21st-century curriculum. In Chapter 2, Ajay Ramful and Sitti Maesuri Patahuddin focus on the implications for school mathematics in the era of the Fourth Industrial Revolution (4IR). This chapter focusses on research within the context of Mauritius and revolves around the extent to which school mathematics prepares students to embrace technology for their career paths. Two key questions guide this chapter, i.e. what are the enablers in the teaching and learning of school mathematics that empower students to embrace the 4IR and how can the school mathematics curriculum be revamped to be aligned to the demands of the 4IR to prepare students for the future.

Chapter 3 by Reginald Gerald Govender is located within the South African context. This chapter focusses on developing a more relevant educational field concerning coding and robotics. The Fourth Industrial Revolution highlights the importance of computer programming, robotics, and data coding, which has prompted educational institutions globally to introduce these fields into the early years of schooling. This chapter presents an ideal curriculum that spans two years and motivates students to use their technology-based tools creatively. The chapter also provides examples of good practice for introducing abstract concepts, for example, programming and robotics to beginners.

Part 2 concerns the 21st-century classroom environment and comprises of two chapters. Chapter 4 by Vimolan Mudaly is situated within South Africa and involves visualization within the era of the Fourth Industrial Revolution. The chapter focused on a qualitative interpretive study with teachers and was framed within the ambits of the Iterative Visualization Cycle. The Iterative Visualization Cycle is an adaptation of Kolb's Experiential Learning Theory. The chapter highlights the voices of the participating teachers to recognize their perceptions concerning visualization within the 4IR. Chapter 5 by Jayaluxmi Naidoo is located within the South African mathematics education context and provides examples of good practice and perceptions of participants on the use of technology-enabled pedagogy in mathematics educational environments. Globally, the findings, as discussed in Chapter 5, have relevance when considering the role of the Fourth Industrial Revolution within educational contexts.

The next three chapters in Part 3 revolve around teachers in the 21st century. In Chapter 6, Septimi Kitta and Jaquiline Amani locate their study within the context of Tanzania. These authors critically focus on assessment within the Fourth Industrial Revolution. The chapter maintains that the 21st-century teacher ought to be lifelong learners and need to apply innovative teaching and assessment approaches that personalize learning while providing students with practical skills. Chapter 7 by Asheena Singh-Pillay focusses on technology education students at a South African Teacher Education institution. This chapter discusses examples of good practice concerning responsive teaching methods to equip future technology education teachers to support these participants in addressing and solve contextual problems faced by society. These examples of good practice intend to support students as they develop critical 21st-century skills. This case study research required technology education students to use the internet of things, to help them as they teach within the era of the Fourth Industrial Revolution. The chapter goes on to discuss the learning experiences of participants when using the internet of things as they engaged with solving local contextual problems. The findings of this qualitative case study have implications for adding knowledge to the field as we prepare teachers to teach Technology Education within an African context in the era of the Fourth Industrial Revolution.

The final chapter in Part 3, Chapter 8, focusses on the use of mobile technologies in mathematics and technology education. In this chapter, the authors,

Asheena Singh-Pillay and Jayaluxmi Naidoo reflect on a South African case study which sought to explore teacher educators' experiences of using mobile technologies. This chapter advances the rationale that teacher educators' pedagogical and technological practices cannot be understood without considering their socio-cultural backgrounds. The findings reveal that teacher educators use mobile technologies to heighten students' awareness of mathematics and technology in everyday life. Thinking is initiated by enabling students to move from the concrete, observable phenomena to the abstract understanding of principles and their applications as they design and solve contextualized problems. The findings of this interpretive case study exhibit that the use of mobile technologies enhances students' observations, discussions and presentation skills. Moreover, the findings highlight that teacher educators' pedagogy relating to mobile technologies are impacted by early learning experiences and socio-cultural background. The findings, as discussed in Chapter 8, have implications for the Technological, Pedagogical and Content Knowledge model and calls for an extension of the model.

The book concludes with Part 4 which includes two chapters on students in the 21st century. Chapter 9 by Yashwantrao Ramma, Ajeevsing Bholoa, Shobha Jawaheer, Sandhya Gunness, Henri Tin Yan Li Kam Wah, Ajit Kumar Gopee and Deewarkarsingh Authelsingh looks at the teaching and learning of science within the Mauritian context. This chapter highlights a study that was conducted to investigate the extent to which science students had developed critical thinking through scientific reasoning at the secondary school level. The chapter further reflects on the subsequent implications for the tertiary level of education in Mauritius. One of the key findings of this Mauritian based study is that science students at secondary and tertiary levels have developed limited critical thinking. This critical thinking is based on their prior knowledge when assessing a given contextual situation and eventually make the appropriate decisions concerning solving problems within the given context. The findings stemming from this study have implications for the teaching and learning of science in the Mauritian and global education systems.

The last chapter in Part 4, Chapter 10 by Jennifer M. Schneider and Guy Trainin, explores the implementation of inquiry-based learning within the ambits of Genius-Hour. Genius Hour is a K-12 classroom project-based learning strategy that was located within an educational context in the United States of America. For this interpretive case study, Jerome Bruner's constructivist learning theory in addition to Daniel Pink and Peter Gray's theory of structured play were combined to establish a concrete framework. With a focus on building a constructivist culture through Dewey's experiential Learning by Doing, Genius-Hour originated as a learning design programme. By fostering inquiry, creativity, research, and collaboration through exploring student-generated questions, Genius-Hour expands project-based/problem-based learning to passion-based learning. The central research question for the study focused on students' perceptions of participating in Genius Hour in the classroom. The themes that were identified from a qualitative analysis of the generated data were independence, support, motivation, and mentorship. Some examples of good practice in the form of artifacts from successful Genius-Hour projects and learning experiences of participants are included in Chapter 10. The authors maintain that through the use of this unique approach to learning and the use of different technologies, teachers and students will become successful 21st-century citizens as they embrace the Fourth Industrial Revolution.

Collectively, the contributions in this book provide not only up-to-date findings but also illustrate the breadth of research on self-directed learning; they provide overviews of the history and evolution of our understanding of this important educational approach; they offer practitioners examples of self-directed learning in diverse contexts, and they suggest directions for further research. Notably, the contributing authors also demonstrate the meaningful changes to student learning that are possible from a collaborative research effort and evidence-based teaching practices. Researchers and educators alike stand to gain much inspiration and many insights into self-directed learning from this book.

Acknowledgments

As the editor of *Teaching and Learning for the 21st Century: Embracing the Fourth Industrial Revolution*, I am grateful to the contributions of all authors. Authors willingly shared their empirical, theoretical research and their philosophies focusing around what it means to teach and learn within the Fourth Industrial Revolution. I am grateful to the peer reviewers for their constructive feedback to ensure a rigorous and double-blinded peer-review process. The international and national peer reviewers gave their time and expertise readily. The idea of initiating this edited volume emanated from research that was supported by the National Research Foundation (NRF) of South Africa: NRF Grant Number: TTK170408226284, UID: 113952. I am grateful to the NRF for supporting my research focusing on embracing the Fourth Industrial Revolution. I am thankful to John Bennett, Henriët Graafland and associates from Brill | Sense for recognizing the value in publishing this edited volume. I am incredibly grateful to my family for always encouraging me to succeed with everything that I undertake. Thank you for supporting my endeavours.

Note

Any findings, thoughts or conclusions described in this edited volume is that of the editor and authors, and no academic or funding institution is answerable for any of the material in this regard.

Figures and Tables

Figures

3.1 The effects of online technology on teaching and learning (adapted from Naidoo & Govender, 2014). 34
3.2 First-year overview of the DK curriculum. 36
3.3 Second-year overview of the DK curriculum. 38
3.4 Four common principles of CT (adapted from Anistyasari & Kurniawan, 2018). 40
4.1 The iterative visualization thinking cycle. 57
4.2 Improving understanding in Algebra 1: A deeper understanding of Algebra/Math (adapted from Chaouki & Hasenbank, 2013). 59
6.1 21st-century teachers' knowledge base: A conceptual framework (based on Anangisye, 2010; Binkley et al., 2012; Care, 2018; Chowdhury, 2016; Daisy, 2015; Kolb, 2014; NIE, 2009; Schleicher, 2012; Rasheed & Wahid, 2018; The American Association of Colleges for Teacher Education [AACTE], 2008; UNESCO, 2008a). 93
8.1 The TPACK framework (adapted from Koehler, Mishra, Akcaoglu, & Rosenberg, 2013, p 3; reproduced by permission of the publisher, © 2012 by tpack.org, http://tpack.org). 124
9.1 Power cut problem. 144
9.2 Outcome in critical thinking. 147
10.1 Katie's To Kill a Mockingbird ceiling tile. 165
10.2 Katie's work in 2019. 166
10.3 Tamara's "Scout" dress on a model. 167

Tables

3.1 Piaget's stages of cognitive development integrated with educational robotics (adapted from Piaget, 1964). 43
7.1 Common elements of the case study for teaching method. 109
9.1 Frequency distribution. 143
9.2 Process of criticality. 145
9.3 Overview of findings from questionnaires 1 & 2. 146
9.4 Average scores of participants in the power cut problem. 147
9.5 Post-hoc analysis (Wilcoxon signed-rank test) for secondary school students. 148
9.6 Post-hoc analysis (Wilcoxon signed-rank test) for tertiary students. 148
9.7 Mann-Whitney U tests. 148

Notes on Contributors

Jaquiline Amani
Senior Lecturer: Education and Psychology: Mkwawa University College of Education: Tanzania. Her publications include a contribution to *Papers in Education and Development* (2019).

Deewakarsingh Authelsingh
Senior Lecturer: Visual Arts Department: Mauritius Institute of Education. His research interests include the use of educational technology in Arts and Design. His publications include *Branding and Identity*, a manual published by Open University, Mauritius (2019).

Ajeevsing Bholoa
Senior Lecturer of Mathematics Education at Mauritius Institute of Education (MIE). His publications include a chapter contributed to *African Virtue Ethics Traditions for Business and Management* (edited by K. Ogunyemi, Edward Elgar Publishing, 2020).

Ajit Kumar Gopee
Lecturer: University of Technology: Mauritius. His publications include a chapter contributed to *Information Systems Design and Intelligent Applications* (Springer, 2019).

Reginald Gerald Govender
Lecturer: Computer Science Education: University of KwaZulu-Natal, SA. His website: http://fibonacci.africa/ offers free coding and mathematics content. His publications include a contribution to *International Journal of Business and Management Studies*.

Sandhya Gunness
Senior Lecturer: Open and Online Learning, University of Mauritius (UoM). She has numerous publications, including a contribution to *ICEL 2018 13th International Conference on e-Learning*.

Shobha Jawaheer
Senior Lecturer: Biosciences and Ocean Studies: University of Mauritius (UoM). She has published widely, including an article in *Biosensors & Bioelectronics*.

Septimi Kitta
Senior Lecturer: Educational Psychology and Curriculum Studies: University of Dar es Salaam: Tanzania. His publications include a contribution to *Advanced Journal of Social Science*.

Vimolan Mudaly
Professor of Mathematics Education at the University of KwaZulu-Natal, South Africa. He has published many articles, including articles in *Journal of Education*.

Jayaluxmi Naidoo
Associate Professor: Mathematics Education at the University of KwaZulu-Natal, South Africa. She has published extensively, including a contribution to *Universal Journal of Educational Research* (2020).

Sitti Maesuri Patahuddin
Lecturer: Mathematics: State University of Surabaya, Indonesia and Assistant Professor: Education: University of Canberra (Australia). Her publications include contributions to *Asia-Pacific Education Researcher*.

Ajay Ramful
Mathematics Lecturer: Mauritius Institute of Education. He has published widely, including contributions to *Mathematics Education Research Journal*.

Yashwantrao Ramma
Professor of Science Education and Head of Research Unit (Mauritius Institute of Education: MIE). He has published extensively, including a contribution to *Science Education in Theory and Practice* (Springer, 2020).

Jennifer M. Schneider
Learner facilitator in Omaha, Nebraska. She is a PhD student at the University of Nebraska-Lincoln in Lincoln, Nebraska, USA. Her publications are included in *EdSurge News*.

Asheena Singh-Pillay
Senior Lecturer: Technology Education (University of KwaZulu-Natal), South Africa. She has published widely including an article in *Journal for the Education of Gifted Young Scientists*.

Guy Trainin
Professor and Chair: Teacher Education at the University of Nebraska-Lincoln, USA. He is widely published including an article in *Contemporary Issues in Technology and Teacher Education*.

Henri Tin Yan Li Kam Wah
Associate Professor: University of Mauritius. He is widely published, including a chapter in *Flagship Universities in Africa* (edited by D. Teferra, Palgrave, 2017).

CHAPTER 1

Exploring Teaching and Learning in the 21st Century

Jayaluxmi Naidoo

Abstract

Within the Fourth Industrial Revolution, society is transforming rapidly. Technology is being swiftly integrated into all aspects of our life. As professionals in education, we need to ascertain whether or not we are adequately prepared for this transformation. Besides, for quality teaching and learning in the 21st century to be provided, it is essential to understand important aspects of teaching and learning in the 21st century. This chapter explores the notions of the Fourth Industrial Revolution and provides an overview of teaching and learning in the 21st century. The chapter goes on to discuss aspects of the 21st-century curriculum; the 21st-century classroom environment; the 21st-century teacher and the 21st-century student. For this chapter, research situated in global contexts have been surveyed to provide the reader with discussions focusing on what it means to teach and learn in the 21st century while incorporating the notions of the Fourth Industrial Revolution. Globally, the discussions in this chapter have relevance when considering the role of the Fourth Industrial Revolution within global educational contexts.

1   Introduction

In recent years novel technologies have led to substantial transformations to our daily lives. We have entered an innovative stage in the history of technological growth and are now in the era of the Fourth Industrial Revolution. Globally, the Fourth Industrial Revolution is envisaged to create new job opportunities and a better society. Embracing the Fourth Industrial Revolution within education contexts is an important issue being researched globally. Within all education contexts, coupled with embracing the Fourth Industrial Revolution are issues of what it entails to teach and learn within 21st-century educational contexts.

For professionals involved in education, there is a need to embrace this transformation. We need to understand that what our jobs are today might be diverse in the not too distant future. Teaching methods are evolving just as rapidly as the industries they serve. Hence we need to equip our in-service and pre-service teachers with the latest innovative and responsive teaching methods. These methods will assist our teacher educators and teachers in preparing their students and learners for the Fourth Industrial Revolution. Therefore, amidst these innovative transformations, as teacher educators and teachers, we need to discern the role that we will play within the Fourth Industrial Revolution.

2   The Fourth Industrial Revolution

The Fourth Industrial Revolution is explained as the assimilation of the physical and virtual world, creating a more globally united society which has changed humanity and the way we live (Schwab, 2016). In the era of the Fourth Industrial Revolution (4IR), the Internet of Things (IoT), robotics, artificial intelligence (AI) and virtual reality (VR) are widespread (Pyper, 2017) and are transforming the way we exist. Thus, as we embark on the 4IR, it is evident that technology will play an important role in nearly all facets of our lives. Moreover, the 4IR involves advanced proficiencies for people and machines and signifies new means in which technology becomes entrenched within society (Schwab, 2016). The swift pace of this change is unsettling industry, society and education in every country since the 4IR has altered the way people subsist. Thus, our education structures must be adapted to prepare students better to succeed in these conditions (Butler-Adam, 2018).

In traditional educational environments, students are situated at desks surrounding one another, however, within the 21st-century educational background, we envision a transformation and that a global real-time interaction will be possible through using the internet and technology-based tools. As professionals within the education sector, we need to welcome this transformation and recognize that what our jobs are today may be altered in the future. Our education systems ought to be reformed to better prepare students for the critical thinking skills and flexibility they will need to succeed in their careers in the future (Butler-Adam, 2018). We ought to enhance the student's ability to problem-solve. Based on critical and creative thinking, problem-solving is essential for flexibility, and this is important for succeeding within the 4IR.

Also, to succeed within the 4IR, an essential method for development would be technology growth (Seck, 2015). To prepare the capacity needed for this growth in technology, education ought to adapt as fast as the demand for Information Communications and Technology (ICT) skills is developing. Students would need to be exposed to and be stimulated to learn through technology-enabled pedagogy and technology-based tools to enhance the development of technology within educational environments. Teachers would also need to be proficient in using technology-enabled pedagogy and technology-based tools. To prepare the required capacity for the 4IR, educational settings ought to adapt quickly since the demand for remote and virtual pedagogy globally is increasing and progressing. Moving forward, this edited volume provides examples and case studies of good practice to support teachers, students and researchers to embrace the 4IR within the 21st-century educational environment.

3 Teaching and Learning in the 21st Century

Ideas about teaching and learning within the 21st century have required a transformation in the educational environment and focusses on 'globalization and internationalization' (Boholano, 2017, p. 22). Teachers and students are required to possess critical skills to achieve success within the 21st-century educational environment. These skills include critical thinking, communication, collaboration, problem-solving and creativity (Fadel, 2008). To gain these skills, teachers need to use innovative learning models where students are provided with the opportunity to engage with activities that foster collaboration, communication, critical thinking, problem solving and creativity. These types of activities encourage students to flourish as they participate and interact on a global platform. When using innovative learning models, it is possible to supplement and enrich traditional pedagogy with multi-media presentations and technology-enabled pedagogy. This transformation in pedagogy supports, facilitates and expands the learning processes and empowers sophisticated levels of student and teacher interaction which scaffolds meaningful teaching and learning (Leow & Neo, 2014).

Apart from transforming pedagogy, to be successful with teaching and learning in the 21st century, it is also crucial for educational environments to be changed accordingly. These transformations need to consider that including technology-based tools within the educational environment is not adequate to supplement a transformed pedagogy. Instead, the educational environment needs to be flexible to inform best practices, and tangible learning spaces need to restructured to support interactive educational environments (Boothe & Clark, 2014). Catering and supporting interactive educational environments also requires curriculum reforms. Curriculum material ought to link content knowledge to real-world applications and problem situations that enable students to perceive how their learning connects with their lives and the world around them, learning should be relevant and realistic for students (Beers, 2011).

3.1 The 21st-Century Curriculum

Education in the 21st century needs to integrate content for various subjects and disciplines as well as skills for the 21st century. The skills that are required to teach and learn in the 21st century successfully include critical thinking, creativity, collaboration, communication, information literacy, media literacy, technology literacy and flexibility (Beers, 2011; Fadel, 2008). Curriculum developers need to revise curriculum material to incorporate the development of these key skills and promote an interactive student-centered educational context (Boholano, 2017). While the effects of technological transformations in education are unspecified, improving digital, communication and collaboration skills are important to allow students to successfully adapt to the transforming future work environments (Bone & Ross, 2019). Skills for the 21st century can support students to flourish in their future careers by scaffolding 21st-century teaching and learning to improve student outcomes (Alismail & McGuire, 2015). Thus, curriculum revision needs to include content material that links crucial knowledge and skills for the 21st century to relevant real-world problems and applications so that students may envision the importance and relevance of what they are learning with aspects of their lives and the real world (Beers, 2011).

Besides, revising curriculum so that there is a link with the real world and authentic situations can enhance student involvement, as well as encourage and motivate students to learn content material while preparing them for the future (Alismail & McGuire, 2015). Also, to use revised curriculum material effectively in the 21st-century educational contexts, teacher development needs to be encouraged. The 21st-century teacher needs to be competent with using innovative technology-based tools and resources since this is an integral part of successful teaching and learning (Jan, 2017). Technology-based tools can enhance student's achievement if used suitably (Sarkar, 2012). Thus, teacher development is essential to ensure that teachers are aware of curriculum revisions, technology-based tools and resources that support teaching and learning in the 21st century. Also, to integrate technology-based tools suitably into teaching and learning in the 21st-century requires that teachers are professionally developed and informed of innovative and emerging technology-based tools and resources (Jan, 2017).

3.2 *The 21st-Century Classroom Environment*

In the 21st century, the classroom environment needs to be arranged so that the classroom is student-centered, not teacher-centered. Teachers in the 21st century need to become facilitators and guides of learning. The main focus of learning in the 21st-century classroom is where students are encouraged to learn by doing. While the student is learning by doing, the teacher is alongside the student as a guide, coaching the students through this interactive learning process. Teachers need to be supported as they make the shift to become guides and facilitators (Jan, 2017) since they are instrumental in helping students as they work on tasks and activities so that learning is not done in isolation. Creating a supportive and safe classroom environment that encourages respect and collaboration supports problem-posing teaching and learning (Murphy, 2010). This is an essential aspect of teaching and learning in the 21st century.

Moreover, the use of ICT in educational contexts supports student-centered learning environment (Sarkar, 2012). Thus, technology-integrated learning in the 21st century enriches and sculpts the educational environment (Boholano, 2017). Also, the 21st-century classroom environment favors the flipped or blended learning approach. The flipped learning approach is a combination of the traditional teaching approach with the integration of technology-based tools and resources when teaching (Ramakrishnan & Priya, 2016). The flipped learning approach entails a transformation in traditional teaching and learning and is grounded on the idea of exchanging in-class teaching time with out of class practice time (Hwang, Lai, & Wang, 2015). Thus, by using the flipped learning approach, students are exposed to content material through videos and presentations before the lesson; hence, the use of technology-based tools are essential in the flipped learning classroom environment.

The blended learning approach combines and promotes both traditional teaching and the use of technology-based tools and resources within the classroom environment (Lalima & Dangwal, 2017). The role of the teacher as a guide or a facilitator is vital within the blended learning environment since this environment enhances and encourages the learning of content material by using both the traditional teaching and learning approach and the integration of technology-based tools into teaching and learning (Jong, 2016). As is evident, technology-based tools are integrated into teaching and learning to support both the student and the teacher and these tools need to be used to help students to access, analyze, organize and share what they are learning. Students need to be provided with the opportunity to select the most suitable technology-based tool for these activities independently (Beers, 2011). These are essential practices to encourage students to develop as they learn within the era of the Fourth Industrial Revolution. Moreover, the classroom environment needs to be transformed to enable students to attain problem-solving, creative thinking and collaboration skills that they require to succeed in their future careers and life (Sural, 2017).

3.3 *The 21st-Century Teacher*

In the 21st century, society is transforming swiftly. Thus, teachers need to acknowledge these changes by preparing their students for the world in which they will live and work in (Larson & Miller, 2011). The skills of critical thinking, creativity, collaboration, communication, information literacy, media literacy, technology literacy and flexibility are important skills that are required for successful teaching and learning in the 21st century (Beers, 2011; Fadel, 2008). Teachers need to be professionally developed to acquire these skills, and they need to be developed further to successfully convey these essential skills to their students (Tican & Deniz, 2018). Technology is an important aspect of daily life in the 21st century (Figg & Jaipal, 2012), as such, teaching in the 21st century also necessitates that teachers use technology-based tools and contemporary teaching resources to teach content material. This signifies that teachers need to use all the necessary resources to make teaching and learning relevant and realistic while incorporating problem-solving and examples from the real world to support and prepare students for the future. The notion of problem-based learning is vital to incorporate within 21st-century teaching and learning (Brears, MacIntyre, & O'Sullivan, 2011) as this is an essential approach for developing independent thinking among students (Bell, 2010).

Moreover, in the 21st century, teachers take on an important role of a facilitator or guide in the educational environment. For example, teachers guide students by using problem-based learning, whereby students attempt problems situated in a real-world context (Wismath & Orr, 2015). Thus, teachers need to make teaching relevant and authentic by promoting thinking skills, encouraging communication, tackling misconceptions, encouraging collaboration and making use of technology to strengthen and promote teaching and learning (Tican & Deniz, 2018). Teachers need to partake in professional development workshops that demonstrate how technology may be integrated into practical teaching and learning educational environments (Figg & Jaipal, 2012). Teacher development workshops often take place in official surroundings, such as teacher training platforms, teaching and research communities, and formal mentoring courses (Timperley, 2011). Teachers may also be involved in professional development through informal collaborations that occur during peer teaching, shared planning, and communications between colleagues (Little, 2012). Additionally, teachers can join ongoing professional development workshops to share 21st-century pedagogic strategies with other teachers and expand their personal technology skills (Kaufman, 2013).

3.4 The 21st-Century Student

Students in the 21st century are independent thinkers and work in collaboration with their peers, the teacher and technology-based tools (Boholano, 2017). Collaborative communication and authentic problem solving are two of the key 21st-century skills teachers want students to develop (Wismath & Orr, 2015). Students in the 21st century have grown up in a predominantly technology-driven society (Boholano, 2017); hence teachers ought to integrate technology into teaching and learning in the 21st century for constructing relevant and realistic educational environments. We need to prepare exciting lessons that motivate and encourage students to learn to ensure positive learning outcomes. This implies that teaching and learning in the 21st century need to cater precisely for the 21st-century student. The diverse educational environments within which the 21st-century students are located needs to be taken into consideration, to ensure that teaching and learning pedagogy is innovative, engaging, thought-provoking, and relevant for the 21st-century student.

For the 21st-century student, expertise in 21st-century skills and knowledge should be the outcome of 21st-century teaching and learning so that students are supported to succeed in their future careers and life (Sural, 2017). Thus, there is a need for students to be efficient when using technology to examine, consolidate, appraise, and communicate information (Larson & Miller, 2011). Also, in the 21st century, students initiate their own learning through problem-based learning, and they work collaboratively to investigate, examine and craft projects that reflect their knowledge (Bell, 2010). Thus, students in the 21st century need to be allowed to explore and foster their own identity (Kaufman, 2013). Promoting student's independent thinking skills develops their active citizenship abilities (Murphy, 2010) which will support students as they prepare for careers in the future. We need to ensure that our future generation of leaders are independent thinkers that can successfully lead society globally.

4 Conclusion

Teaching and learning in the 21st century while acknowledging the notions of the Fourth Industrial Revolution (4IR) brings about exciting opportunities and experiences. Based on the discussions in this chapter, it is evident that global evidence-based research revolving around examples of good practice and authentic case studies on how we teach and learn in the era of the 4IR provides one with much to think about. Ideas on how to transform the curriculum and classroom environment for the 21st century, as discussed in this chapter are important for teachers and curriculum developers to consider. Also, the role of the 21st-century student and teacher is essential to contemplate to achieve success with teaching and learning in the 21st century. As teachers, teacher educators, students, curriculum developers and researchers, we can learn from the discussions in this chapter by adapting or expanding on them. We are in the era of the 4IR, and the value of 21st-century skills for teaching and learning is inexhaustible. The 21st-century teacher ought to be comfortable with the use of technology-enabled pedagogy within their educational environments, and teachers need to be proficient at using 21st-century skills and knowledge within their teaching. The 21st-century teacher needs to be adept at conveying these critical 21st-century skills and knowledge to their students to better prepare their students for work and life in the future. Globally, these discussions have relevance when considering the role of the Fourth Industrial Revolution within 21st-century educational environments.

References

Alismail, H. A., & McGuire, P. (2015). 21st century standards and curriculum: Current research and practice. *Journal of Education and Practice, 6*(6), 150–155. https://files.eric.ed.gov/fulltext/EJ1083656.pdf

Beers, S. Z. (2011). 21st century skills: Preparing students for their future. *STEM: Science, Technology, Engineering and Mathematics*, 1–6. https://cosee.umaine.edu/files/coseeos/21st_century_skills.pdf

Bell, S. (2010). Project-based learning for the 21st century: Skills for the future. *The Clearing House, 83*(2), 39–43. doi:10.1080/00098650903505415

Boholano, H. B. (2017). Smart social networking: 21st century teaching and learning skills. *Research in Pedagogy, 7*(1), 21–29.

Bone, E. K., & Ross, P. M. (2019). Rational curriculum processes: Revising learning outcomes is essential yet insufficient for a twenty-first-century science curriculum. *Studies in Higher Education, 1*(1), 1–12. https://www.tandfonline.com/doi/epub/10.1080/03075079.2019.1637845?needAccess=true

Boothe, D., & Clark, L. (2014). *The 21st century classroom: Creating a culture of innovation in ICT*. https://conference.pixel-online.net/ICT4LL/files/ict4ll/ed0007/FP/0475-ICL733-FP-ICT4LL7.pdf

Brears, L., MacIntyre, B., & O'Sullivan, G. (2011). Preparing teachers for the 21st century using PBL as an integrating strategy in science and technology education. *Design and Technology Education, 16*(1), 36–46. https://ojs.lboro.ac.uk/date/article/view/1588

Butler-Adam, J. (2018). The Fourth Industrial Revolution and education. *South African Journal of Science, 114*(5), 1. https://doi.org/10.17159/sajs.2018/a0271

Fadel, C. (2008). 21st Century skills: How can you prepare students for the new Global Economy? In *Partnerships for 21st century skills*. https://www.oecd.org/site/educeri21st/40756908.pdf

Figg, C., & Jaipal, K. (2012). *TPACK-in-practice: Developing 21st century teacher knowledge*. Paper presented at the Society for Information Technology & Teacher Education International Conference, Austin, Texas, USA. https://www.learntechlib.org/p/40349/

Hwang, G., Lai, C., & Wang, S. (2015). Seamless flipped learning: A mobile technology-enhanced flipped classroom with effective learning strategies. *Journal of Computers in Education, 2*(4), 449–473. https://doi.org/10.1007/s40692-015-0043-0

Jan, H. (2017). Teacher of 21st century: Characteristics and development. *Research on Humanities and Social Sciences, 7*(9), 50–54. https://www.researchgate.net/profile/Hafsah_Jan/publication/318468323_Teacher_of_21_st_Century_Characteristics_and_Development/links/5977688ba6fdcc30bdbad40d/Teacher-of-21st-Century-Characteristics-and-Development.pdf

Jong, J. P. (2016). The effect of a blended collaborative learning environment in a Small Private Online Course (SPOC): A comparison with a lecture course. *Journal of Baltic Science Education, 15*(2), 194–203.

Kaufman, K. K. (2013). 21 ways to 21st century skills: Why students need them and ideas for practical implementation. *Kappa Delta Pi Record, 49*(2), 78–83. doi:10.1080/00228958.2013.786594

Lalima, D., & Dangwal, K. L. (2017). Blended learning: An innovative approach. *Universal Journal of Educational Research, 5*(1), 129–136. doi:10.13189/ujer.2017.050116

Larson, L. C., & Miller, T. N. (2011). 21st century skills: Prepare students for the future. *Kappa Delta Pi Record, 47*(3), 121–123. doi:10.1080/00228958.2011.10516575

Leow, F.-T., & Neo, M. (2014). Interactive multi-media learning: Innovating classroom education in a Malaysian university. *The Turkish Online Journal of Educational Technology (TOJET), 13*(2), 99–110.

Little, J. W. (2012). Professional community and professional development in the learning-centered school. In M. Kooy & K. van Veen (Eds.), *Teaching-learning that matters: International perspectives* (pp. 22–46). Routledge.

Maphosa, C., & Mashau, S. T. (2014). Examining the ideal 21st century teacher-education curriculum. *International Journal of Educational Sciences, 7*(2), 319–327.

Murphy, T. (2010). Conversations on engaged pedagogies, independent thinking skills and active citizenship. *Issues in Educational Research, 20*(1), 39–46. http://www.iier.org.au/iier20/murphy.pdf

Pyper, J. S. (2017). Learning about ourselves: A review of the mathematics teacher in the digital era. *Canadian Journal of Science, Mathematics and Technology Education, 17*(3), 234–242. doi:10.1080/14926156.2017.1297509

Ramakrishnan, N., & Priya, J. J. (2016). Effectiveness of flipped classroom in mathematics teaching. *International Journal of Research-Granthaalayah, 4*(10), 57–62. doi:10.5281/zenodo.192292

Sarkar, S. (2012). The role of Information and Communication Technology (ICT) in higher education for the 21st century. *The Science Probe, 1*(1), 30–40.

Schwab, K. (2016). *The Fourth Industrial Revolution* (pp. 172). World Economic Forum.

Seck, A. (2015). Technology production: A challenge for economic growth and development in Africa. *Journal of African Studies and Development, 7*(8), 207–214. doi:10.5897/JASD2015.0356

Sural, I. (2017). 21st century skills level of teacher candidates. *European Journal of Education Studies, 3*(8), 530–538. https://oapub.org/edu/index.php/ejes/article/view/949/2731

Tican, C., & Deniz, S. (2018). Pre-service teachers' opinions about the use of 21st century learner and 21st century teacher skills. *European Journal of Educational Research, 8*(1), 181–197. https://files.eric.ed.gov/fulltext/EJ1203100.pdf

Timperley, H. (2011). *Realising the power of professional learning*. McGraw-Hill Education.

Wismath, S. L., & Orr, D. (2015). Collaborative learning in problem-solving: A case study in metacognitive learning. *The Canadian Journal for the Scholarship of Teaching and Learning, 6*(3), 1–17. https://files.eric.ed.gov/fulltext/EJ1084619.pdf

PART 1

The 21st-Century Curriculum

CHAPTER 2

The Fourth Industrial Revolution: Implications for School Mathematics

Ajay Ramful and Sitti Maesuri Patahuddin

Abstract

In this reflective chapter, we undertake a mapping exercise from the anticipated demands arising from the Fourth Industrial Revolution to the foreseeable mathematical readiness and disposition incumbent on our secondary school students. Industry 4.0 is categorized by the increasing automaticity and interoperability of production systems which are becoming extensively data-driven. As technologies are developed within Industry 4.0, they also become available as by-products for the field of education, changing the rules and norms of learning. An immediate concern is an extent to which school mathematics is preparing our youngsters to develop a mindset that can embrace these technologies and be ready for new jobs that we may not have considered. We attempt to provide anticipative answers to the following two questions: (i) What are the enablers that can nurture the appropriation of the affordances of Industry 4.0 in the teaching and learning of school mathematics? (ii) How should the school mathematics curriculum be revamped to align it to the demands of Industry 4.0 and develop the incumbent dispositions in preparation for future vocational and functional obligations? To answer the two questions, firstly, we review steps that have already been initiated to accommodate the tools of Industry 4.0 in the domain of mathematics education. Secondly, as a didactic exercise, we map out the mathematical skills that new technological frontiers may require in light of projected developments. We also pre-empt some of the challenges that this new revolution may engender such as resistance to changes from influential stakeholders and changes in teachers' mindset and preparation. We use the knowledge gathered in mathematics education as a backdrop to chart a trajectory that can potentially embody the new technologies from Industry 4.0 into our discipline.

1 Introduction

What is taught and learnt at schools, is to a considerable extent dictated by the needs of the individuals, the society and the needs of industries as economic drivers of the society. These needs change as the society evolves and new artifacts and ways of operating add to the fabric of humankind. In particular, mathematics education as a discipline has grown noticeably in terms of the content and processes taught in schools. For instance, arithmetic was a major focus of school mathematics at the beginning of the 20th Century and emphasized drilling and rote learning (Kilpatrick, 1992). Similarly, logarithm tables were an integral part of the mathematics curriculum. Today, arithmetic is taught in ways that are focused more on sense-making with the support of technology. Calculators have replaced the Logarithm tables.

Similarly, in the past students had to know a range of theorems and their proofs in geometry, especially for examination purposes. Today, geometry, as a practical domain, is much more valued through exploration, especially with the availability of geometrical software. Moreover, Computer Algebra Systems (CAS) and Graphical software are opening new possibilities for learning mathematics through dynamic exploration in visually-rich environments (Birgin & Acar, 2020; Thomas, Monaghan, & Pierce, 2004).

Over the last two decades, the content of the school mathematics curriculum has remained focused on those elements that are considered fundamentals, i.e., Numbers, Algebra, Geometry, Measurement, Probability and Statistics, staggered progressively from elementary through to secondary school. What has changed, are the resources and tools available to learn mathematics as well the teacher is not the main source of knowledge. As teacher educators, researchers working with school children, and curriculum developers, we are in a privileged position to sense the evolution of mathematics teaching and learning. The body of knowledge accumulated in the field of mathematics education over the years (e.g., English, 2008; Grouws, 1992) has emanated from research and practical wisdom concerning teaching and learning, assessment practices, curriculum challenges, and the penetration of technology in the discipline.

Undeniably, technology is engendering a turning point in the field of mathematics education. Mathematics may no longer be a paper-and-pencil activity for many students as the digital learning environment overwhelms them with learning resources and opportunities. It is a fact of life that students are heavily dependent on smartphones and can readily access the wide repertoire of resources at their own choice and pace, beyond the confinement of the teacher-controlled environment (Nayak, 2018). The teaching-learning paradigm has changed where the teacher is not the sole authority of knowledge, but where students also are involved in knowledge production, altering the way we teach and learn. New technologies are expanding the boundaries of the classroom beyond space and time, and there is deeper symbiotic interaction between man and machines (Demartini & Benussi, 2017). The technological transformations are bringing new job markets, calling for a new set of skills for today's youth. What are the implications of these technological changes with regards to school mathematics?

2 Industry 4.0 and Related Work in Mathematics Education

We first circumscribe a workable boundary around the essential constituents of Industry 4.0 to be able to develop our arguments for the implications that such technologies may have for the mathematics teacher, curriculum developer and the learner. Even before the arrival of the Industry 4.0 era, the array of technological concepts was already overwhelming with ideas such as virtual mathematics learning (Moyer, Salkind, & Bolyard, 2008), mobile learning (Motiwalla, 2007), and ubiquitous learning (Hwang, Tsai, & Yang, 2008).

Now with the arrival of Industry 4.0, it is becoming even more daunting to determine the possibilities that such new waves of development may engender. Essentially, the Fourth Industrial Revolution is characterized by Cyber-Physical Systems (CPS) and the Internet of Things (IoT), Cloud technologies, Robotics, Artificial Intelligence (AI), Augmented Reality (AR), Virtual Reality (VR), 3D printing, and Computational Thinking (CT) as a critical skill necessary to handle the tools of Industry 4.0 (Baygin, Yetis, Karakose, & Akin, 2016). Next, we briefly explain each key element of Industry 4.0, comment on its relation to mathematics education and highlight the benefits it can provide for the new generation of learners.

3 Cyber-Physical Systems and the Internet of Things

Cyber-Physical Systems (CPS) are integrations of computational systems with physical world processes, where computer algorithms control physical objects, processes or systems. As pointed out by Gleason (2018): "CPSs are computer-based algorithms that work with physical processes in which embedded computers and networks monitor and control the physical processes of machines and artificial intelligence (AI) in a feedback loop whereby one informs the other" (p. 146).

A related concept is the Internet of Things (IoT) which refers to the networking of physical devices or systems including wireless connections, cloud technologies, embedded sensors and actuators that allow gadgets to collect and send real-time data (Aheleroff et al., 2020). IoT enables the integration of STEM disciplines as students collect physical, chemical, or physiological data from their environment through sensors and actuators (e.g., via a school-based weather station). This information is directly connected to students' digital footprints which allow them to process authentic data for investigation.

Thus, the IoT provides opportunities for immersing students in mathematically-meaningful situations so that they find value in learning. Importantly, students can see the connection between mathematics and the sciences. As highlighted by Kusmin (2019), in 'Smart Schoolhouse by means of IoT', the Internet of Things offers many prospects that encourage inquiry-based learning to engage students with real-life situations. However, the full potential of IoT is yet to be explored in investigative and analytic activities among school students.

It is expected that there will be growing connection between computational objects and physical systems, and this will change the workplace, where workers will be more involved in developing and managing automated systems (Waschull, Bokhorst, Molleman, & Wortmann, 2020). We foresee two categories of future workers: frontline users who will embark on professional jobs directly related to Industry 4.0 and end-users, who will use the products of Industry 4.0 and by extension need some form of mathematical knowledge. Experience shows that only an insignificant minority of students undertake advanced studies in Mathematics while the majority tend to be consumers of mathematics.

Undeniably, the frontline users of Technology 4.0 will require robust problem-solving skills, computer programming, data processing skills and optimization knowledge. Together with the technical knowledge and skills, the frontline users will have to display an inquisitive frame of mind and character of audacity to engage in solving novel problems collaboratively as they tackle unpredictable problems in quest of innovation and increasing automation.

Whatever the configuration and complexity of new manufacturing production systems, the human operator of these systems need a set of essential skills that can be sourced back to school mathematics. The knowledge and skills that one acquires in school mathematics constitute the foundation on which the talented worker will construct his/her mathematical toolkit for operating the technologies of Industry 4.0. Therefore, at best, the mathematics school curriculum must ensure that workers have a problem-solving attitude beyond mastering concepts and procedures. Each worker must develop confidence in handling mathematical information and appreciate the relevance of the discipline as a service subject in the workplace.

4 Artificial Intelligence

Essentially, Artificial Intelligence (AI) is regarded as systems which are intelligent agents that can perceive external data and use the ensuing information to perform particular tasks intelligently. AI provides multiple possibilities for the creation of intelligent artefacts for the teaching and learning of mathematics (Gadanidis, 2017). These interactive platforms do not only provide explanations of mathematical concepts and principles or help in problem-solving, but they interact responsively to students' needs.

5 Robotics

Robotics (e.g., VEX robots, LEGO Mindstorms) as an activity is already being used in schooling systems to support students understanding of the connection between Science, Technology, Engineering and Mathematics (STEM) (Sisman, Kucuk, & Yaman, 2020). Robots as automated motorized learning devices provide students opportunities to understand scientific and engineering principles in action and to enact mathematical concepts (Leoste & Heidmets, 2019; Samuels & Haapasalo, 2012). In their review of literature on the potential of educational robotics in mathematics education, Zhong and Xia (2020) found that although the research evidence shows that Robotics engages students in interactive and hands-on activities, results are quite inconclusive regarding the benefits for mathematics learning.

6 Augmented Reality

Augmented Reality (AR) adds virtual elements to our real environment and allows us to superimpose different pieces of information, enabling enhanced visualization. It permits the interaction of the physical and virtual world, allowing previously intangible concepts to be integrated into the visual learning environment. AR is gaining research attention in mathematics education at both elementary and secondary school level (e.g., Fernández-Enríquez & Delgado-Martín, 2020; Tomaschko & Hohenwarter, 2019).

AR has potential applications in the teaching of abstract concepts both in pure and applied mathematics and provides affordances to 'give life' to concepts and processes, thus potentially helping students to make sense of mathematics. By combining virtual reality with real-world elements, AR offers many possibilities for mathematics educators to create contextual situations without having to leave the class. Indeed, it will require much creativity and imagination to harness the possibilities that AR offers for the teaching and learning of school mathematics, especially with enhanced visualization affordances (Conley, Atkinson, Nguyen, & Nelson, 2020; Fernández-Enríquez & Delgado-Martín, 2020).

With advances in technology, it is predicted that AR software will become more user-friendly and accessible to teachers. AR remains an object of interest to Mathematics educators as it offers possibilities for students' engagement in an attempt to increase learning gains and interest in mathematics.

7 Three Dimensional Printing

Mathematics educators have recognized the potential of three dimensional (3D) printing, where students create 3D objects from geometrical designs rather than start with physically-build 3D objects. The 3D printing activities involve the creation of solid objects that require the integration of knowledge and skills from different areas (e.g., design, the science of materials, computer science and mathematics) (Budinski et al., 2019). They provide a rich medium for enhancing visualization skills as students design objects using 3D modelling programs and observe the result of their creation in the finished solid material object.

The usefulness of 3D printing in enhancing spatial reasoning in non-geometry-based areas such as Calculus is yet to be fully explored. 3D printing also enlarges the teachers' toolkit by creating opportunities to integrate project-based learning in the teaching of mathematics. Importantly, 3D printing allows students to experience the integration of Science, Technology, Engineering and Mathematics (Ng, 2017). In their study involving hand-held 3D printing technology, Ng and Ferrara (2020) assert that the learner mobilizes artefacts to perform mathematically thus, affording students opportunities to produce knowledge rather than merely consuming knowledge. The job market is already calling for talents in additive manufacturing and reverse engineering, using computer-aided design and 3D scanners for the production of objects. Thus, giving students some early experiences through school mathematics may create much inspiration for this relatively novel area of human creation.

8 Computational Thinking: A Critical Skill for Industry 4.0

Computational Thinking (CT) is regarded as a set of problem-solving skills encompassing screen-based coding, digital tangibles such as programming of robots and off-screen algorithms (Gadanidis, 2017). It is a skill-set that is required in almost all the sectors of Industry 4.0. It entails elements such as algorithmic thinking, programming, models and simulations, data analysis and system thinking. Mathematics provides the context to develop CT skills, giving students the opportunity to formulate problems amenable to computer-based solutions. CT enriched experiences were found to impact mathematics problem-solving performance among 15-year olds (Costa, Campos, & Guerrero, 2017). According to Costa et al. (2017), the intervention provided some starting points for the integration of CT in the mathematics curriculum. They illustrate how conventional school mathematics problems can be reformulated so that they align with CT. Another concept related to CT is Big Data analytics, especially with the colossal amount of data available through online sources and mobile technologies. Big Data analysis requires a thorough grounding in statistics and computing and is becoming increasingly important in business, marketing and communication industry, creating new career opportunities.

The key to embedding CT in the mathematics curricula is through problem-solving, which is one of the fundamental process standards of school mathematics. In their attempt to promote open-ended problems, curriculum developers may include CT-oriented exploratory activities as an integral part of textbooks. At the same time, mathematics educators may be motivated to consider this form of activities in their teacher preparation programs. Further, a new research agenda should be opened for the study of CT in mathematics education in the era of Industry 4.0 to create interest and give traction to this form of mathematical modelling and analytical thinking (English, 2018).

What are the common denominators from the different components of Industry 4.0 that are appealing to the field of mathematics education? These are exploratory possibilities which offer spaces for experiential learning and enhanced visualization features for making mathematical concepts more accessible to students. The integration of knowledge from different areas which enable the applicability of mathematics to be visible and opportunities for creativity and innovation also provides problem-solving pathways in authentic contexts. The qualities brought to the fore by Industry 4.0 supports what mathematics educators have been advocating for a long time, that school mathematics should have a project-based element and prioritize authentic learning experiences. Industry 4.0 provides a medium to change the face of school mathematics from a mere accumulation of facts, conventions and principles, as is often the case, to applications and creative endeavors.

The Fourth Industrial Revolution is upon us and challenging curriculum developers, teachers, and policymakers to adapt to the flow of teaching and learning possibilities sourcing from CPS and IoT, Artificial Intelligence, Robotics, Augmented Reality and 3D printing. From a technological point of view, what is foreseen in this revolution is higher gigabit exchange capabilities, enhanced cyber-physical systems, enhanced interactivity, a higher level of virtual elements, and more extended and automated functionalities from AI so that machines second human activities. It is also suggested that there will be "a fusion of technologies that is blurring the lines between physical, digital, and biological spheres" (Schwab, 2016, p. 1).

Despite the fast-changing progress in technological advances, their integration in teaching and learning have followed a quite subdued pace. Such disparities can be explained by several factors ranging from cost considerations to their acceptance in the educational milieu. It may not be an exaggeration to say that the tools in Industry 3.0 are yet to be exploited to enhance the teaching and learning of mathematics, although Industry 4.0 is already here. These observations are the rationale for the first question that we address in this chapter.

9   Results and Discussion

9.1   *Enablers That Nurture the Appropriation of the Affordances of Industry 4.0 in the Teaching and Learning of School Mathematics*

We make the argument for three critical enablers with regards to the processes that can facilitate the integration of the tools of Industry 4.0 in the teaching and learning of mathematics. Enabler 1 focuses on policymaking, Enabler 2 spotlights teachers and teaching, while Enabler 3 considers learners and learning.

9.1.1   Enabler 1: Mandatory or Statutory Integration of New Tools in the Mathematics Curriculum

We are already in the presence of multiple tools from Industry 3.0 that we are yet to harness for the teaching and learning of mathematics. As a case in point, Microsoft Excel is a highly valuable tool for the teaching and learning of statistics at the secondary school level and is readily available (Bernard, Minarti, & Hutajulu, 2018). However, only a handful of teachers tend to use it, although it is user-friendly, and is aligned to conventional school syllabus pertaining to descriptive and inferential statistics.

What may explain the reluctance of teachers to use exploratory investigations through Excel in their statistics classes? How do logistic, administrative or accountability constraints limit the use of technological tools? We contend that as long as these tools are not officially written in curriculum documents to get a mandatory or statutory status and are associated with assessment, their use may be in jeopardy. We substantiate this view from the fact that the calculator has become an integral part of the curriculum as its use is an attribute of assessment procedures.

In a centralized and exam-oriented education system, the mathematics curriculum is quite loaded, and there is much emphasis on performance, leading teachers and students to prioritize practice exercises in the form of test papers. Teachers are thus working in some form of survival mode where they have to complete many topics within a prescribed time. Thus, the system of education and its underlying accountability mechanisms may condition the state of mind of teachers.

9.1.2 Enabler 2: Addressing Teachers' Disposition and Readiness to Explore the New Products of Industry 4.0 and Their Fit for Purpose

Building the state of mind of teachers is as important as the content knowledge for teaching. In our teacher education programs, we come across participants with different predispositions, some inclined to experiment with new ideas. In contrast, others are fixed on their approaches, especially those who have already had several years of teaching experience. How do we cope with a mindset to enable the experimentation and the adoption of new tools for Industry 4.0?

Our small-scale, school-based projects have led us to conclude that teachers tend to implement initiatives if they fit their values and the practical requirements of their jobs. Technological tools in education may have only a honeymoon effect and may not be sustained over time. The products of innovation are sustainable not only if they are fit for purpose, but also if teachers are willing to invest time and resources in their adoption. For schools to adopt the products of Industry 4.0, they must be willing to give curricular time to such activities and get the sponsorship of the school administration that espouses a liberal view and values innovation.

As mathematics educators, we are on a continuous lookout for ways of improving the teaching and learning of mathematics. We attempt to keep up with technological innovations. Although technology is an integral part of our teacher education programs, we admit that more needs to be done at our level to embrace the opportunities from the tools of Industry 4.0. Universities and teacher education institutions need to deploy more leadership and innovative capabilities to bridge the affordances of Industry 4.0 in teacher education programs. As teachers build their teaching philosophies during their training programs, they should be exposed to rich experiences from technological affordances such as AR, Robotics, 3D printing, and the IoT. This may assist in appreciating the inherent virtues and potentially shape their values and teaching practices. Our experiences show that once teachers develop their bedrock conceptions of mathematics, it is quite challenging to effect teacher change. Hence, it is critical to tune teachers to technological affordances early when they are in their training programs.

9.1.3   Enabler 3: Fostering Appropriate Habits of Mind: Problem-Solving Attitude, Perseverance, Resilience, and Independent Learning

Besides policy, curriculum and teaching, it is also important to focus attention towards students who are the final recipients of the new modes of learning. Schooling experiences are pivotal in shaping students' preparedness, interest and passion for the choices that they make with regards to their careers. To what extent are school mathematics experiences preparing students to embark, adapt and thrive in the Fourth Industrial Revolution (4IR)? Are the content and processes used to teach mathematics, enabling students to develop an exploratory mindset and problem-solving attitude?

Project-Based Learning (PBL) has continuously been considered as a rich pathway to encourage students to problem solve in authentic situations. For instance, 3D printing, as a STEM-oriented Industry 4.0 technology, offers many affordances for engaging students in authentic problem-solving situations (Ng, 2017). Also, 3D printing enables students to develop their creativity as they use their knowledge of Geometry and Calculus in action. By playing with equations, they can generate solids that can be printed and hence appreciate solids of revolution, for instance. They can generate a paraboloid by rotating the curve $y = x^2$ along the y-axis and print the resulting 3D solid with these tools. Children can see the concrete embodiment of mathematical concepts and the application of mathematics in the resolution of authentic problems. The possibilities that 3D printing offers as a learning tool is only starting to unfold.

Initiating students to the tools early enough not only exposes them to the inherent affordances but also have inspirational values. At a later point, when students join the job market with their background school experience, they may not be confronted by a new, unfamiliar world. As researchers in mathematics education, our experience suggests that children can be very creative; it's just a question of providing the appropriate tools and the necessary enabling environment.

Another feature of a problem solver that is highly advocated in mathematics education is perseverance or resilience (Williams, 2014). It is important to engage students in challenging or non-routine problems so that they get the experience to explore novel situations and develop persistence. As they work through problem situations and look for viable pathways to overcome obstacles, they are prompted to undertake some form of deep thinking. We foresee that the type of novel problems that future employees will be handling in Industry 4.0 will be complex and multifaceted. Schooling should provide students with some insight into challenging situations and help them to develop perseverance with underlying self-concept and self-esteem as problem solvers. The pace with which Industry 4.0 is evolving requires every individual to be a lifelong learner. Another requisite skill in the Industry 4.0 era is self-regulation, that is individual competencies to set goals and tasks, plan approaches to the tasks, monitor the process, evaluate the outcomes, and reflect on the process and solutions (Zimmerman, 1990).

Furthermore, exposing students to what current developers of Industry 4.0 are doing may also bring some stimulus to show what they can achieve with their mathematical knowledge. The secondary school and world-of-work alliance are important to create the impetus for students to see the prospects in future jobs and also the necessity for 'thinking big'. Exposure to the job prospects may motivate students to develop particular inclinations for mathematics as they may appreciate that it offers the toolbox to thrive in Industry 4.0 and is associated with more than a decent salary.

9.2 *Revamping the School Mathematics Curriculum to Align with the Demands of Industry 4.0 and Prepare for Future Vocational and Functional Obligations*

Our first question addressed the processes and system capabilities that may facilitate the appropriation of the tools of Industry 4.0 in mathematics teaching and learning. In the second question, we reflect on the content of school mathematics and address the issue of the adequacy of the current curriculum. Contemporary school mathematics, across several education systems, tend to focus on Numbers, Algebra, Measurement, Geometry, Probability and Statistics and to some extent, aspects of Calculus. In our role as curriculum developers, often we have to decide what to include or exclude in school mathematics, taking into consideration what we want learners to achieve at the end of the school cycle.

As we make space for Industry 4.0 in the mathematics curriculum, we are faced with several critical questions: (i) What weight are we willing to attribute to Industry 4.0 in the mathematics curriculum?; (ii) What additional elements to include in the curriculum and at the expense of what content due to an already overloaded curriculum?; (iii) How should we streamline the new content across the elementary and secondary school level?; (iv) What content do we assume to be accessible to elementary and secondary school students and what is more appropriate for university?; (v) Is there a different way of reorganizing the mathematics curriculum to enable the integration of Industry 4.0? The answers to these questions vary across cultures as a function of value systems. The economy (depending on whether a country has the money to invest in industry 4.0 technologies) and economic orientations (depending on the directions in which the economy of a country is being steered) of a country is of importance.

We attempt to provide some pointers to the above questions by looking at the type of mathematical knowledge that is required in Industry 4.0. A diverse set of technical mathematical knowledge is necessary to handle the tools of Industry 4.0: Mathematical Modelling, Game Theory, Number Theory, Cryptography, Numerical Analysis, Differential Equation, Numerical/Scientific Computing, Linear Algebra, Matrix Theory, Networks, Operations Research and Optimization, Statistics, Probability, Simulation and Logic, among others (Formaggia, 2017). It would be too demanding and unproductive to systematically work backwards from the mathematical knowledge required for Industry 4.0 and extract elements that can be staggered over the school mathematics curriculum. Rather it may be more practical to isolate core content that provides the foundational skills across domains and is related to the current mathematics curriculum. To that end, computational thinking is the first element that may provide some pointers to develop skills consonant to the exigencies of Industry 4.0. Traditionally, school mathematics curricula tend to provide students with primarily computational and problem-solving experiences. It is also important to proactively introduce students to algorithmic thinking as a first step to automation. Engaging students in coding experiences will set the first step to programming and simulation.

The second aspect is data analysis which has already received extensive consideration in mathematics education (Gal, 2002; Watson, 2013). However, more traction is necessary to elevate the teaching of statistics in the school mathematics curriculum. Students should be given practical experiences to process real data, especially with the new possibilities offered by the IoT. They should be given adequate experiences to develop the competence to handle data, small as well as large data sets, as they build their repertoire and confidence.

The third aspect that can open a viable pathway to build Industry 4.0 readiness is mathematical modelling which has been theoretically and practically debated in mathematics education (Li, 2013). In school mathematics, students do get some experiences with mathematical modelling in domains such as algebra, functions (e.g., exponential growth) and differential equations (e.g., rate of change). Mathematical modeling involves a broad range of areas, and it may be wise to choose some pertinent ones (e.g., optimization) that are more directly relevant to Industry 4.0. It should be noted that the intention is not to fragment skills in the learning process but to identify some starting points for encouraging students to develop a mathematical mindset commensurate with Industry 4.0 requirements.

We have suggested three-pointers that may serve as orientations to make the school mathematics curriculum more responsive to the call from Industry 4.0. The idea is not to bring every piece of requisite mathematical competency from Industry 4.0 to secondary school but to expose students to experiences that may highlight the potential of mathematics in solving an array of problems, using the knowledge and skills that they develop at school. The intention is also to create a learning environment that enables the enculturation of work habits, dispositions, and the confidence to meet the requirements of the world of work. An ancillary aim is to inspire students to develop affinities for career trajectories other than the traditional ones associated with medicine, engineering, law, science, agriculture, humanities and similar areas. Secondary schools may be the privileged space where students are shaping their career orientations.

If the school mathematics curriculum cannot accommodate the changes that are being proposed to enable the integration of the tools of Industry 4.0, we suggest a new secondary school subject is introduced with the intent of promoting 'STEM Practices' (Lowrie, Leonard, & Fitzgerald, 2018). The concept of STEM Practices emerged as a way to highlight the underlying idea, methods and values common across STEM domains (such as creativity, teamwork, and problem-solving) that will be vital in transitioning to the world of Industry 4.0. It is anticipated that this subject will create more space for dedicated work in terms of Project-Based Learning. An industry-school alliance may be initiated so that people who are already in the technical professions share their practices with secondary school students. It is important to take aggressive steps at the secondary school level itself to increase the likelihood for observable results in terms of participation and engagement in CPS, Robotics, AR, 3D printing and new areas such as digital twin technologies. Implementing school-based initiatives may avoid scarcity of knowledge and skills to fuel Industry 4.0 in the long run.

10 Conclusion

The modern world is constantly being challenged by global competitiveness, the massification of activities, fast-cycling of human operations and climate change. Also, modern society is characterized by an increasing materialistic form of living. As a result, industries are responding to emerging challenges for economic sustainability. It is thus becoming more than necessary to make optimal use of resources, develop resource-saving strategies and importantly automate manufacturing processes. Thus, new technologies are being created to sustain the society, with technological innovations being one of the most viable and efficient options.

In consequence, the nature of the labor force is changing and requires new skills. In this wave of changes, schools are being pressured to reinvent themselves to better respond to the needs of individuals and society. Mathematics education, as a discipline, has started to respond to these challenges, although much more remains to be done.

In this chapter, we have brought to the fore the enablers that tentatively may help to overcome the barriers to allow the optimal use of the tools of Industry 4.0. By no means is the transformation of school mathematics linear, as we decide which elements of technology to incorporate into existing curriculum and how they should be implemented to bring added value to school mathematics in preparation of Industry 4.0.

It is important to keep pace with the innovations taking place in Industry 4.0 so that we can elevate the field of mathematics education. Industrialists are finding ways to work collaboratively in the appropriation of Industry 4.0 (Standards Australia, 2017). Similarly, educators need to be engaged in more collective debates in terms of an agenda for actions. Also, more empirical research is required to validate the learning gains from applications such as IoT, Robotics and 3D printers. At this stage, answers to questions of the robustness of concept acquisition through these technologies are quite tentative.

Likewise, another key question is whether these new ways of engaging with mathematics through the latest tools and resources lead to better learning of mathematics. Many key questions remain open: Who decides what to include in the mathematics curriculum in response to technological innovations? How to sensitize policymakers on the issue? At what stage should the new tools of Industry 4.0 be included in the curriculum? What could be some feasible bridging mechanisms? How to reconfigure the school mathematics curriculum to give space to the tools of Industry 4.0 with much fidelity? Are examination boards ready to consider alternative forms of assessment provided that the demonstration of learning may be quite different from the tools of Industry 4.0?

Technology may take time to gain acceptance among educators, especially if it does not squarely fit the expectations of educators. Teachers have established routines of work, and shifting out of that comfort zone may not be straightforward. Understandably, designers of technology are market-oriented, and their tools may not always be designed for ready use by educators. For instance, many educators are fascinated by 3D printing, yet it has several imperfections that need to be addressed. To that end, designers and mathematics educators must work cooperatively so that they better serve each other in their innovative and practical endeavors. The level of sophistication of the tools of Industry 4.0 may be intimidating for educators, and some works may be necessary to get teachers on board. A new era is unfolding, and mathematics educators should give full attention to the affordances of Industry 4.0, as this may be an opportunity to innovate and make a turn in the culture and practice of school mathematics.

References

Aheleroff, S., Xu, X., Lu, Y., Aristizabal, M., Velásquez, J. P., Joa, B., & Valencia, Y. (2020). IoT-enabled smart appliances under industry 4.0: A case study. *Advanced Engineering Informatics, 43*, 101043.

Baygin, M., Yetis, H., Karakose, M., & Akin, E. (2016, September 8–10). An effect analysis of industry 4.0 to higher education. In *2016 15th International Conference on Information Technology Based Higher Education and Training (ITHET)*. IEEE. https//doi.org/10.1109/ITHET.2016.7760744

Bernard, M., Minarti, E. D., & Hutajulu, M. (2018). Constructing student's mathematical understanding skills and self-confidence: Math game with visual basic application for Microsoft Excel in learning Pythagoras at junior high school. *International Journal of Engineering & Technology, 7*(3.2), 732–736.

Birgin, O., & Acar, H. (2020). The effect of computer-supported collaborative learning using GeoGebra software on 11th grade students' mathematics achievement in exponential and logarithmic functions. *International Journal of Mathematical Education in Science and Technology*, 1–18. doi:10.1080/0020739X.2020.1788186

Budinski, N., Lavicza, Z., Vukić, N., Teofilović, V., Kojić, D., Erceg, T., & Budinski-Simendić, J. (2019). Interconnection of materials science, 3d printing and mathematic in interdisciplinary education. *STED Journal, 1*(2), 21–30.

Conley, Q., Atkinson, R. K., Nguyen, F., & Nelson, B. C. (2020). Mantaray AR: Leveraging augmented reality to teach probability and sampling. *Computers & Education*, 1–22. https://doi.org/10.1016/j.compedu.2020.103895

Costa, E. J. F., Campos, L. M. R. S., & Guerrero, D. D. S. (2017). *Computational thinking in mathematics education: A joint approach to encourage problem-solving ability.* Paper presented at the 2017 IEEE Frontiers in Education Conference (FIE).

Demartini, C., & Benussi, L. (2017). Do Web 4.0 and industry 4.0 imply education X.0? *IT Professional, 19*(3), 4–7.

English, L. D. (Ed.). (2008). *Handbook of international research in mathematics education*. Lawrence Erlbaum Associates.

English, L. D. (2018). On MTL's second milestone: Exploring computational thinking and mathematics learning. *Mathematical Thinking and Learning, 20*(1), 1–2.

Fernández-Enríquez, R., & Delgado-Martín, L. (2020). Augmented reality as a didactic resource for teaching mathematics. *Applied Sciences, 10*(7), 1–19.

Formaggia, L. (2017). Mathematics and Industry 4.0. Retrieved June 2, 2020, from https://www.researchgate.net/publication/321155366

Gadanidis, G. (2017). Artificial intelligence, computational thinking, and mathematics education. *The International Journal of Information and Learning Technology, 34*(2), 133–139.

Gal, I. (2002). Adults' statistical literacy: Meanings, components, responsibilities. *International Statistical Review, 70*(1), 1–25.

Gleason, N. W. (2018). Singapore's higher education systems in the era of the Fourth Industrial Revolution: Preparing lifelong learners. In N. W. Gleason (Ed.), *Higher education in the era of the fourth industrial revolution* (pp. 147–148). Springer Nature.

Grouws, D. A. (Ed.). (1992). *Handbook of research on mathematics teaching and learning*. Macmillan Publishing Co.

Hwang, G.-J., Tsai, C.-C., & Yang, S. J. (2008). Criteria, strategies and research issues of context-aware ubiquitous learning. *Journal of Educational Technology & Society, 11*(2), 81–91.

Kilpatrick, J. (1992). A history of research in mathematics education. In D. Grouws (Ed.), *Handbook of research on mathematics teaching and learning* (pp. 3–38). Macmillan.

Kusmin, M. (2019). *Inquiry-based learning and trialogical knowledge-creation approach in smart schoolhouse supported by IoT devices*. Paper presented at the 2019 IEEE Global Engineering Education Conference (EDUCON).

Leoste, J., & Heidmets, M. (2019). The impact of educational robots as learning tools on mathematics learning outcomes in basic education. In *Digital turn in schools – Research, policy, practice* (pp. 203–217). Springer.

Li, T. (2013). Mathematical modeling education is the most important educational interface between mathematics and industry. In A. Damlamian, J. Rodrigues, & R. Sträßer (Eds.), *Educational interfaces between mathematics and industry* (Vol. 16, pp. 51–58). Springer.

Lowrie, T., Leonard, S., & Fitzgerald, R. (2018). STEM practices: A translational framework for large-scale STEM education design. *EdeR. Educational Design Research, 2*(1), 1–20.

Motiwalla, L. F. (2007). Mobile learning: A framework and evaluation. *Computers & Education, 49*(3), 581–596.

Moyer, P. S., Salkind, G., & Bolyard, J. J. (2008). Virtual manipulatives used by K-8 teachers for mathematics instruction: The influence of mathematical, cognitive, and pedagogical fidelity. *Contemporary Issues in Technology and Teacher Education, 8*(3), 202–218.

Nayak, J. K. (2018). Relationship among smartphone usage, addiction, academic performance and the moderating role of gender: A study of higher education students in India. *Computers & Education, 123*, 164–173.

Ng, O.-L. (2017). Exploring the use of 3D computer-aided design and 3D printing for STEAM learning in mathematics. *Digital Experiences in Mathematics Education, 3*(3), 257–263.

Ng, O.-L., & Ferrara, F. (2020). Towards a materialist vision of 'learning as making': The case of 3D printing pens in school mathematics. *International Journal of Science and Mathematics Education, 18*, 925–944. https://doi.org/10.1007/s10763-019-10000-9

Samuels, P., & Haapasalo, L. (2012). Real and virtual robotics in mathematics education at the school–university transition. *International Journal of Mathematical Education in Science and Technology, 43*(3), 285–301.

Schwab, K. (2016). *The Fourth Industrial Revolution*. Crown Business.

Sisman, B., Kucuk, S., & Yaman, Y. (2020). The effects of robotics training on children's spatial ability and attitude toward STEM. *International Journal of Social Robotics*, 1–11. https://doi.org/10.1007/s12369-020-00646-9

Standards Australia. (2017). Industry 4.0: An Australian perspective – Recommendations report to the Australian Government – Department of Industry, Innovation and Science.

Thomas, M. O., Monaghan, J., & Pierce, R. (2004). Computer algebra systems and algebra: Curriculum, assessment, teaching, and learning. In K. Stacey, H. Chick, & M. Kendal (Eds.), *The future of the teaching and learning of algebra, the 12th ICMI study* (Vol. 8, pp. 153–186). Springer.

Tomaschko, M., & Hohenwarter, M. (2019). Augmented reality in mathematics education: The case of GeoGebra AR. In T. Prodromou (Ed.), *Augmented reality in educational settings* (pp. 325–346). Brill Sense.

Waschull, S., Bokhorst, J., Molleman, E., & Wortmann, J. (2020). Work design in future industrial production: Transforming towards cyber-physical systems. *Computers & Industrial Engineering, 139*, 1–11. https://doi.org/10.1016/j.cie.2019.01.053

Watson, J. M. (2013). *Statistical literacy at school: Growth and goals*. Routledge.

Williams, G. (2014). Optimistic problem-solving activity: Enacting confidence, persistence, and perseverance. *ZDM, 46*(3), 407–422.

Zhong, B., & Xia, L. (2020). A Systematic review on exploring the potential of educational robotics in mathematics education. *International Journal of Science and Mathematics Education, 18*(1), 79–101.

Zimmerman, B. J. (1990). Self-regulated learning and academic achievement: An overview. *Educational Psychologist, 25*(1), 3–17.

CHAPTER 3

Embracing the Fourth Industrial Revolution by Developing a More Relevant Educational Spectrum: Coding, Robotics, and More

Reginald Gerald Govender

Abstract

The dawn of industrial revolution 4.0 requires the creation of a new educational spectrum that includes teaching and learning content, as well as educational theories that are responsive and relevant to the post-Digital Age. This calls for a modification to seminal theories to enable a successful 21st-century era of teaching and learning. Using Information and Communication Technology devices such as digital projectors, slides, clickers; and smartboards are fairly outdated in the current education sector. The introduction of tablet personal computers and apps, together with learning and classroom management systems, has become a favored pedagogical tool. We have witnessed a global movement towards apps that has resulted in educators being encouraged to use tablets in innovative ways, to enhance the learning experience. The advantages of such innovation can only be realized when students are adept at using digital tools, and when educators integrate the tools meaningfully into their pedagogy.

Industrial Revolution 4.0 is emphasizing the significance of computer programming, robotics, and data coding, which has prompted many education departments globally to introduce these fields into the early years of schooling. These fields produce skills that are not only relevant to the time that we live in but influence the future and economic growth of countries. It is crucial that these skills are developed and nurtured at the primary level. This chapter presents an ideal curriculum that spans two years and ignites a desire in students to use their tablet innovatively. It also explores some innovative pedagogic tools and techniques based on literature and personal experience, as well as provides ways to introduce abstract concepts like programming and robotics to novices. The approaches probed herein are from a South African context, with the focus on content characteristics, impact, and importance.

1 Introduction

1.1 Educational Robotics and Coding

Effective learning is a result of active teaching and largely depends on the teachers' effective practices (Furner & Kumar, 2007). The fascination with robotics and coding in education started with the work of South African born mathematician and computer scientist Seymour Papert (Papert, 1980). His curiosity about gears at an early age, together with the educational influence of working with Jean Piaget in later years, led him to be a pioneer in educational robotics and coding. Robotics, coupled with intelligent systems in the Fourth Industrial Revolution (IR 4.0), has shone new light onto this work.

Embedded Artificial Intelligent (AI) systems, together with Machine Learning (ML), allow for real-time decision making. This plays a pivotal role in the advancement and neural activities of humankind. AIs have the potential to direct you with precise turns to and from work or provide suggestions for eating out in an unfamiliar area based on past visits to restaurants. Search engines are becoming more powerful and accurate in analyzing millions of data points that you enter, in turn making personal suggestions that offer an artificial sense of caring and attention, all thanks to Big Data. The possibility of quantum computing, moving away from bits to quantum bits,[1] provides quantum mechanics functionality such as superposition or entanglement to perform computation (Heaney, 2019). The possibilities of complex digital systems in education have the potential to be fruitful (Luckin et al., 2016), but can also pose pitfalls (Pierce & Hathaway, 2018). However, this chapter focuses on the positive attributes of innovative pedagogies that involve technologies of the 4IR[2] era, and how they respond to current educational needs.

1.2 Global Change in Education

Education has become a global priority to meet the demands of the post-Digital Age,[3] thus leading to the focus on robotics and coding, which has resulted in swift curriculum changes in the early schooling years. Along similar lines, the South African President, Cyril Ramaphosa, stated during the State of Nation Address (SONA) that, "with our Framework for Skills for a Changing World, we are expanding the training of both educators and students to respond to emerging technologies including the internet of things, robotics and artificial intelligence" (SONA, 2019, p. 25). Countries for example, the United States of America, the United Kingdom, and Australia are further ahead in the implementation process (Kim, 2016), while countries such as Japan and South Africa are still in the planning and implementation phase (Sano, 2019; SONA, 2019).

This global educational transformation towards coding and robotics is referred to as the Digital Education Revolution (Kim, 2016), which feeds into countries' workforces, digital economies, and futures. Teaching and learning activities at schools are changing with the use of Personal Computer (PC) tablets, which offers e-books over hardcopy textbooks and the use of the Internet over physical libraries (Reynolds, 2011). Technology has influenced a global shift in how education is enacted and how the current generation adapts to and views life.

1.3 The Time Line

During this transitional period into IR 4.0, it is important to reflect on the sequence of events that led us to this time. The first industrial revolution took place around 1765 with the introduction of steam power (Musson & Robinson, 1959). The second followed in 1870 with electricity and assembly line production, while the third revolution heralded electronics and computers in 1969 (Philbeck & Davis, 2019). Each revolution took place over a significant number of years and was marked by extraordinary achievements by humankind. Also, humanity's cognitive ability and innovative skills were pushed to higher limits. Klaus Schwab first announced IR 4.0 at the World Economic Forum (WEF) meeting in 2015 (Schwab, 2016), which resulted in people's growing awareness of the current revolution. 4IR intends to emphasize and develop uncharted and exciting technological phenomena, among them AI, Big data, Internet of Things (IoT), and Robotics. So what does this mean for education, specifically teaching and learning?

Education 4.0, a manifestation of Industry 4.0, references a period of new educational paradigms and technologies. Educational technologies are always improving, and it is inevitable that the technologies discussed in this chapter will be upgraded with advanced tools that promise a better teaching and learning experience. Take for example, the wooden pointer and blackboard around the 1850s (Muttappallymyalil et al., 2016), with the promise of gauging students' attention in following what the teacher says on this writing surface. The pencil in the 1900s (Coles, 1999) allowed each student to write without the worry of messy and drying up ink. The teaching machine entered the education market in the 1940s (Skinner, 1958), an invention by psychologist and behaviorist, Burrhus Frederic Skinner. Skinner's teaching machine prompted the user to complete sentences and brought about the programmed instruction movement. Then televisions entered the market with the promise of no teacher required as students watched the lessons onscreen (Bates, 1988). The World Wide Web (www),[4] invented in 1893 by Tim Berners-Lee (Albertazzi & Cobley, 2013), paved the way to Silicon Valley,[5] with the rise of social media and tech giants like Facebook, Instagram, and Google. They are constantly developing advanced tools[6] for the educational sector.

1.4 *Making Education Relevant*

The appropriate integration of new technologies into education plays a pivotal role in keeping education systems relevant relative to global benchmarks. The embracing of IR 4.0 in education will yield knowledge and skills aligned with changing industrial needs. A closer introspection on the appropriate methods of integration raises concerns surrounding students' engagement in the learning process, the achievement of better grades in school, and the volume of enrollment at higher education institutions.

In this post-Digital Age, students need to pursue knowledge which they construct as opposed to memorizing it.[7] This is what I refer to as *attendance for tests*, meaning the student attends the academic intuition to rote learn and write tests. This is similar to what Paulo Freire terms the *banking concept*, where the teacher deposits knowledge into the students' heads as one might deposit money into a bank account (Hilty, 2018). Students in this scenario tend to take on a spectator role in their education process, thus withholding their full cognitive ability. Therefore, the teacher needs to create opportunities for students to become active participants in their knowledge-building process. This would result in dialogue that is necessary to counteract the predominance of *attendance for tests*.

2 Methodology

This is a descriptive chapter based on a literature review, to reveal the current situation of IR 4.0 on education, focusing on coding and robotics together with personal experiences. Data obtained were evaluated by the researcher and interpreted based on a descriptive approach (Buyukozturk et al., 2010). Freire's educational principle underpinned the theoretical considerations that education should lead to transformative action, which serves to liberate humans (Freire, 2018; Shor & Freire, 1987). Thus, the role of education is not limited to the accumulation of knowledge but also the ability to change an individual's life. Aligned to the Freire's educational principle, the work of Piaget and Papert is significant. As Piaget mainly focused on the development of how knowledge systems evolve (Brainerd, 2003) while Papert advocated the use of physical manipulatives in building understanding (Ackermann, 2004). Together with knowledge systems and building understanding need to co-exist to unleash the full potential of the human mind.

2.1 *The Use of Online Technologies*

Real-time communication and collaboration enabled by the Internet of Things (IoT) offer convenient on-the-go services to users whereby different devices are connected via the Internet. Examples of such devices are surveillance systems, geysers, washing machines, smart motor cars and traffic lights. It is anticipated that IoT together with the development of 5G networks,[8] will drive the Internet future to the edge (Li et al., 2018). Fifth-generation (5G) networks promise to deliver data at extremely high speeds with low to zero latency offering real-time computing; thus, for example, delicate medical surgeries can be conducted where the patient and surgeon are on different continents (Gatouillat et al., 2018). Access to and development of the Internet has changed the way we work, learn, and play.[9] To utilize the Internet to the fullest, learning content must enable self-reflection, with or without the presence of the teacher.

Educational online technologies, when designed and implemented effectively, can lead to self-regulation, which in turn leads to learner-centered[10] education (Naidoo & Govender, 2014). Learner-centered education is considered a powerful experience as the student is in charge of their learning path (Hannafin & Hannafin, 2010), resulting in the formation of rich knowledge through a liberal learning process.[11] Many countries, such as South Africa have adopted the philosophical underpinnings of a learner-centered education curriculum. Research conducted by Naidoo and Govender (2014) established a three-way relationship between *online technologies, self-regulation* and *learner-centered education*. Although this research was based on Mathematics,[12] the core goal of any online activity should ultimately mimic the relationship shown in Figure 3.1.

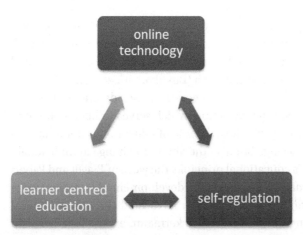

FIGURE 3.1   The effects of online technology on teaching and learning (adapted from Naidoo & Govender, 2014)

In Figure 3.1, the teacher adopts the facilitative approach so that learning can still occur in their absence. The Cognition and Technology Group at Vanderbilt promotes the use of hints or embedded data[13] to serve as support in the absence of the facilitator (Naidoo & Govender, 2019). Hints offer guidance to the student when they reach a mental roadblock. Thus, the learning process becomes increasingly autonomous, giving individual students attention when requested.

The advancements presented by 4IR are centered on only Science, Technology, Engineering and Mathematics (STEM) subjects. However, in understanding the effects on STEM, a harmonious relationship should exist between the STEM subjects and subjects in the Humanities whereby psychological factors and development of cognitive skills related to STEM subjects call upon the knowledge of Humanities for interpretation and understanding.

2.2 *Digital Kingship: A PC Tablet Curriculum*

The availability of educational apps on mobile devices is useful in the learning environment. However, students must be well skilled in using the device. Here, I present an ideal PC tablet curriculum that was successfully implemented in Grade 8 and Grade 9 at a school in Durban, South Africa. Digital Kinship[14] is an eight pillar, two-year curriculum. The lesson comprised of a single 45-minute period allocated once in a seven-day cycle.[15] BYOD (Bring Your Own Device) was applied, where parents selected a device based on their affordability. The use of tablets[16] is an appropriate educational tool for high school students and is also a stationery requirement. The rolling out the curriculum in Grades 8 and 9 benefited students when they reached Grades 10, 11 and 12, as they were able to concentrate on their specialized subjects.[17] In later grades, they would have gained mastery of the device and have the ability to use discipline-specific apps to complete assignments, classwork, homework etc.

Modules were divided into one module per school term or two modules per semester, in a year. First-year modules selected were *ICT policy*, *Classroom Management System (CMS)*, *Getting to know your device*; and *Basic office processing* (Figure 3.2).

Explaining the rules of using the PC tablet at school is important, and includes students and teachers. All stakeholders of the institution must play a part in drafting an ICT policy that applies best to the level of usage of the device. The existing school code of conduct would be an ideal starting point when drafting this policy. The policy must include repercussions for cyberbullying,[18] internet trolling, identity theft, etc. The final document must be submitted for approval to the Education department. This policy forms part of the first module of Digital Kingship, *ICT Policy*.

The second module is a *show and do*[19] module, whereby the teacher facilitates guided exercises through the Content Management System (CMS) or

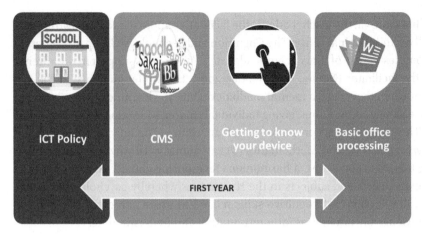

FIGURE 3.2   First-year overview of the DK curriculum

Learning Management System (LMS).[20] The criteria for a successful management system is a good network setup (Roy et al., 2018). Students should be on a separate secure network from staff, for security reasons.

Choosing the ideal CMS can be a challenge, as there are many companies competing in the education technology industry. Moodle, BlackBoard, Chamillo, Canvas and Google classroom[21] are a few systems, amongst others, that can be implemented. Criteria to be considered when selecting a system:
- Cost of the system (monthly and yearly fees),
- Support structure/availability,
- Security,
- Maintenance,
- The technicality of the system – Creating, Reading, Updating and Deleting (CRUD),
- GUI and friendliness of the system; and
- Features and options.

2.3   Getting to Know Your Device

This is the third module, which can be done earlier. The fourth module covered in the first year is *Basic office processing*. This module is crucial as the students need a wide variety of applications that offer notes, highlighting, bookmarks, etc., as well as the basics of typing, creating a presentation and performing simple calculations.

2.4   Content Covered in Each First-Year Pillar
2.4.1   ICT Policy
- Look at global ICT policies,
- Acceptable User Policy (AUP),

- End-User Licence Agreement (EULA),
- Draw focus to the policy do's and don'ts,
- Debit system and consequences if policy not followed; and
- Bring Your Own Device (BYOD).

2.4.2   CMS
- What is the CMS/LMS?
- Login and profile setup; and
- Explore features (uploading, downloading, etc.).

2.4.3   Getting to Knowing Your Device (PC-Tablet)
- Taking care of your device (battery charging, screen protectors, finding device apps, lock/pin protections, etc.),
- Buttons on the device (shortcuts, re-booting device, etc.),
- The five touch screen gestures (Swipe, Pinch, Expand, Tap, Drag and drop),
- Android/iOS versions (history, compatible, etc.),
- Camera (video audio recording),
- Serial numbers, what is International Mobile Equipment Identity (IMEI) and Mobile Equipment Identifier (MEID) numbers? Why are they important? How do I find these numbers?; and
- Features common to all devices (connecting the WI-FI, silent mode, adjusting systems settings, and know-how to execute CRUD – Create, Read, Update and Delete).

2.4.4   Basic Office Processing
- How to type documents/memos/PowerPoint etc. on device,
- MS Office vs Polaris vs Kingssoft and other relevant apps,
- Creating, saving, editing, deleting; and
- Software applications associated to formats: .docx, .pdf, .pptx etc.

On completion of the first year, activities can be given to the students, such as video stories, interviews, presentations or typing an assignment. Teachers must be able to create such learning opportunities for students on the PC-tablets.[22]

The second-year starts with *e-Communication*, after which the teacher and students can communicate in a non-face-to-face manner.[23] The sixth module is *Google play*, to aid the downloading of subject-specific apps. The module *Cybercrime* creates awareness among students about online criminal operations. The last module is *Getting certified*, which summarizes the important concepts covered during the two years. Additional concepts, such as future developments,[24] can be included in this module.

FIGURE 3.3   Second-year overview of the DK curriculum

On completion of Digital Kinship, the student should be able to use their PC tablet to its full potential, without interruptions, to enhance their knowledge building process.

2.5   *Content Covered in Each Second-Year Pillar*
2.5.1   e-Communication
– Explore different methods of communication,
– Internet vs Intranet,
– Setting up an email,
– Netiquette,
– Pros and cons of e-communication,
– Do's and don'ts; and
– Social networking – dos and don'ts of Twitter, Facebook, etc.

2.5.2   Google Play/App Store
– Explore useful Apps,
– Apps that must be on the device (a prerequisite for each subject at school),
– Installing and uninstalling apps,
– Storage capacity, RAM requirements and other system requirements; and
– Backing up apps (Android application packages).

2.5.3   Cybercrime
– Hackers vs crackers,
– Illegal uses of a tablet that leads to a criminal act,
– Examine national and international law on computer crimes,

- Cyberbullying (Who to contact? What to do?),
- Identity theft-spyware; and
- Trolls, malware, phishing, rootkits, spam, Trojans.

2.5.4   Getting Certified
- What does it mean to be a digital citizen?
- My digital footprint,
- Cover anything new and relevant; and
- Recap.

2.6   *Hour of Code*
Introducing students to computer science through computer programming[25] is currently at the forefront of educational reformation. Some countries have developed content-specific courses, while others include coding in general technology subjects or courses (Falloon, 2016; Moreno-León, Robles, & Román-González, 2016). Government-driven initiatives such as *Computer Science for All* in the United States of America, *Computing at School* in the United Kingdom, and *Digital Technologies* in Australia, have one common goal: to promote coding and technologies to students. South Africa will introduce a new subject that will include coding and robotics. The President of South Africa, in his annual State of the Nation Address in 2019, stated that "at the center of all our efforts to achieve higher and more equitable growth, to draw young people into employment and to prepare our country for the digital age, must be the prioritization of education and the development of skills" (SONA, 2019, p. 23).

Alongside the curriculum reform by educational departments towards IR 4.0 fields, several movements are promoting coding and robotics,[26] such as the Hour of Code campaign.[27] This campaign started in 2014 and promoted the creation of one hour of code every day. Hour of Code is an online program which develops one's interest in coding at any age, reaching millions of users who engage in code learning at anytime, anywhere in the world.

2.7   *Computational Thinking*
The technologically driven era we are living in demands that individuals harness their cognitive skills, such as logic and problem-solving. Computational Thinking (CT) provides the essential knowledge, skills and attitude for solving problems encountered in our daily lives (Curzon, 2015). Computational Thinking was first cited by Papert and later made famous by Jeannette Wing, who defined it to apply to multiple disciplines and not only to Computer Science (Kalelioglu et al., 2016). CT can be described as a set of thinking processes that

helps individuals to formulate solutions to problems and can be used in different disciplines (Liu & He, 2014; Wing, 2006). Papert (1980, p. 3) states that "contact with the computer has not, as far as we are allowed to see in these episodes, changed how these people think about themselves or how they approach problems". CT is considered a method for understanding human behavior through problem-solving, designing systems, and developing the basic concepts of computer science (Korkmaz et al., 2016), thus making it a key skill for 21st-century education. Computer programming and other STEM-related subjects can be regarded as subsets of Computational Thinking and not the other way around.

There is no clear-cut definition for CT (Denning, 2017; Voogt et al., 2015). Presented in Figure 3.4 are the four common principles associated with computational thinking.

FIGURE 3.4   Four common principles of CT (adapted from Anistyasari & Kurniawan, 2018)

Attention is drawn to algorithmic design,[28] which is an important problem-solving skill for understanding, applying, and producing algorithms. Algorithmic design or thinking is a process of attaining a solution through defined steps. Important to note is that algorithmic thinking is related to mathematics. However, it is not limited to mathematics (Romero et al., 2017).

A thinking skill like CT is crucial with the increasing global requirement of data analytics and Big Data, which will aid the future workforce. Alike Jacob et al. (2018) assert that the future successful workforce requires multiple levels of abstract thinking, and dynamic solutions for difficult problems, thus *computational thinking* is a necessity.

2.8   *Humanoids*

A set of relationship rules, termed by Issac Asimov the 'laws of robotics', is applied to the interaction between robots and humans:

- Law Zero: A robot may not harm humanity, or, by inaction, allow humanity to come to harm,[29]
- Law one: A robot may not injure a human being or, through inaction, allow a human being to come to harm,
- Law two: A robot must obey orders given it by human beings except where such orders would conflict with the First Law, and
- Law three: A robot must protect its own existence as long as such protection does not conflict with the First or Second Law (Abrahm & Kenter, 1978).

Although these laws were introduced in his 1942 short story *Runaround*, it can be ascertained that they are quite relevant in the 21st century. Humanoids are robots that resemble human beings with high interactive bodily autonomy. In 2014, Softbank mobile from Japan collaborated with a French company, Aldebaran Robotics, to create the first humanoid named Pepper, who could assist humans by reading and responding to human emotions. Sophia was developed in 2016 by Hansen Technologies and was the first robotic artificial intelligence system to gain citizenship of a country[30] (Kalra & Chadha, 2018; Weller, 2017). This was a grand achievement where humans were able to converse with autonomous robots, and allowed deep learning or deep neural networks[31] to be attested to.

India was the first country to endorse a humanoid robot named Eagle 2.0[32] to replace a teacher in one of their schools, allowing for two-way interaction between human students and a robot teacher (Ullas, 2019). The teacher would readily respond to student's questions, as it possessed a bank of knowledge. Drone technology has advanced from basic toy drones to sophisticated flying machines. Tech and e-commerce company, Amazon,[33] are planning to implement drone delivery systems for online orders (D'Onfro, 2019). This delivery system will have positive impacts, such as reduced carbon emissions,[34] reduced waiting times, 24/7 delivery, and the company is likely to no delivery costs because gas is not required; thus resulting in happier customers. This is just one of the many cases where the technologies of IR 4.0 is changing the way we do things.

2.9   *Robots and Education*

Teachers and practitioners of education have access to a wide variety of educational robotics they can use. An exceptional robotic kit to have in class is the Lego Mindstorm series. Based on my own experience, it is difficult to source funds to purchase robotic equipment, since it is generally expensive. Arduino and Raspberry Pi are cheaper alternatives to costly kits like Mindstorm or Tinker-Bots. Simulation software is a cost-effective solution if there are no funds at all.[35] Educational robotics are learning tools that adopt a hands-on learning experience,[36] thus proving ideal for project-based learning, as they incorporate coding, computational thinking and engineering skills or the integration of all these.

There is no definitive guide to integrating robotics into lessons. However, the teacher must find meaningful ways to include the robot, together with its electronic components like sensors and actuators in the existing subject matter. Transdisciplinary STEM education is widely understood as an educational approach that integrates Science, Technology, Engineering and Mathematics (Gerlach, 2014). Although educational robotics may seem more pertinent to STEM-related subjects, there are opportunities to integrate these tools with non-STEM subjects such as social studies, literacy, music and art. Technology allows the students to express themselves, promotes problem-solving and enhances critical thinking.

2.10 The DNA of a Robotics Curriculum

Papert's research focused on how students engage using tools and media, which results in self-directed learning (Ackermann, 2004). In contrast, Piaget was less interested in the use of tools and media and focused on how knowledge systems evolve (Brainerd, 2003). Piaget's stages of cognitive development consist of four fundamental stages (Piaget, 1972). These stages are meaningfully mapped against the use of available educational robotic technologies in Table 3.1. Piagetian theory best suits the introduction of these technologies to younger students. It is worthy to point out that Jean Piaget and Seymour Papert worked together, and the work of these prestigious educationalists is integrated here (Table 3.1).

2.11 Some Educational Robotic Curriculums and Competitions

– WaterBotics (http://waterbotics.org/) is an underwater robotics curriculum for middle and high school students developed by the Stevens Center for Innovation in Engineering & Science Education;
– RoboParty (http://www.roboparty.org/en/) is a robotics camp organized at Universidade do Minho in Guimarães Portugal by Professor A. Fernando Ribeiro, his students, and staff;
– RoboCupJunior (RCJ) (robocupjunior.org) is an educational robotics initiative that promotes STEM learning, coding, computational thinking, and engineering skills with hands-on, project-based and goal-oriented learning through an educational robotics competition;
– First Lego League (FLL) (http://www.firstlegoleague.org/) is an international competition where teams are introduced to scientific and real-world challenges and are required to solve them using Lego robotics; and

TABLE 3.1 Piaget's stages of cognitive development integrated with educational robotics (adapted from Piaget, 1964)

Piaget's stages of cognitive development	Level	Skill	Software[a]	Hardware[b]
Sensorimotor (0–2 years)	Pre-primary	Matching, order, rearranging	–[c]	Lego blocks
Preoperational (2–7 years)	Early years of primary school	Adding order to programs, following steps, block-based programming	codeSpark Academy, Scratch Jr, Kodable[d]	Sphero, Lego We Do, Kibo, BeeBots
Concreate operational (7–11 years)	Late years primary school	Implementing various orders to advanced programs, block-based programming	Scratch, App Inventor, Bits box, Kodu Game Lab, Alice	Lego Mindstorm, Cubelets, Bioloid, OzoBot
Formal operational[e] (11 years and older)	High school and beyond (some might have been exploited earlier)	Text-based programming, programming for real-life scenarios	Delphi Embarcadero, Netbeans, JGrasp, PyCharm	Arduino, Rasberry Pi, Vex iQ

a Software is program or programs controlling the operation of a computer or micro processes.
b Hardware: Physical component that can be connected to a computer system.
c At this age it would not be ideal to introduce the use of software.
d The use of software should be introduced in later years of say 5.
e The formal operation stage is key to abstract thought and metacognition.

– World Robotic League (WRL) (https://worldroboticsleague.com/) is a robotics competition for students of all ages to participate using a variety of Robotics Kits.

3   Conclusion

This chapter has presented an overview of some of the innovative technologies of the 21st century that can be incorporated into one's pedagogic practice. This stemmed from theoretical research mainly informed by the works of Freire (2018), Papert (1980) and Piaget (1972). Attention is given to coding and robotics, as these fields are central to IR 4.0. The world is changing rapidly, influenced by technological advancements. The dawn of IR 4.0 is creating a ripple effect on education. Thus it is essential to highlight topics like coding and robotics, which are paramount skills to ensure students' future success.[37]

It would seem that the processing power available in the 4IR era will accelerate the entry of 5IR, as humanity has accessed quantum computing power, and has created autonomous humanoids that react to human emotions. With this surge of technology, it is crucial to prepare future generations to be highly analytically minded. Computational Thinking will, therefore, be beneficial to students and teachers alike, as it encompasses algorithmic design, problem-solving and logical skills that can be adapted to many disciplines. This thinking is an all-in-one cognitive ability that promotes the future success of our students from an early age and should be integrated into the school curriculum.

A tabulated overview of recommended software and hardware tools based on Piaget's theory (Piaget, 1972) gives the teacher an idea of possibilities, concerning the core focus taught at each grade when introducing robotics and coding. The teacher should seize every opportunity possible to integrate educational robotics into the subject matter. The online platform is making learning (e-learning) convenient, with higher speeds and a variety of content to meet students' learning requirements. Together with a PC tablet, the latter provides an e-learning environment that is portable and easily accessible. However, students must familiarize themselves with the tablet. Digital Kingship's two-year curriculum creates an ideal introduction to motivate students to learn while gaining mastery of this educational tool.

It is observed that many initiatives are driving the importance of coding and robotic applications in schools globally. South Africa is aligning itself with the 4IR era. Recent government interests are piloting ways to integrate coding and robotics into the primary school curriculum. South Africa has started initiating digital education revolution processes; however, time will reveal the success of these initiatives.

Notes

1 Also known as qubits. A bit can be 0 or 1, but qubits can take on an infinite number of values. Read about Holevo's theorem, for further understanding.
2 Fourth industrial revolution (IR 4.0).

3   The Digital Age or Information Age started around the 1970s with the introduction of the personal computer. Read more: https://techcrunch.com/2016/06/23/the-three-ages-of-digital/
4   The first website built was at CERN, France, and was live on the August 1991. It is still operating and can be visited at http://info.cern.ch/hypertext/WWW/TheProject.html
5   An area in San Francisco that is a hub for high technology, innovation, and social media.
6   Both Facebook and Google have created Augmented reality (AR) and Virtual Reality (VR) headsets.
7   Rote learning.
8   Some countries like Japan and Switzerland have acquired active 5G networks since mid-2019.
9   Internet user live statistics: https://www.internetlivestats.com/
10 In this chapter the word learner is reference to student and vice-versa.
11 Not a one size fit all stance.
12 Visit http://fibonacci.africa/ to experience interactive applets base on math and computer concepts.
13 The hints are crucial when planning an online activity and can take the form of text, video, voice notes, etc.
14 The name Digital Kingship refers to the rank a person who is digitally/ICT competent. One who completes the course, has completed the rite of passage to e-learning and is deemed ICT literate.
15 Time tabling system.
16 Tablet is a portable PC whose primary interface is a touch screen.
17 Focus of specific knowledge.
18 Cyberbullying is an electronic form of online bullying or harassment and teenagers are common victims of such crime.
19 Students will follow the teachers actions step by step.
20 Difference between CMS and LMS: CMS is a more passive application, which is mostly used to view documents. CMS is sometimes referred to Classroom Management System. Whereas LMS (Learning Management System) is an application where students are motivated to be interactive with the system for example taking a quiz. Creators are able to create a quiz and track progress of students.
21 Google classroom is free: https://classroom.google.com
22 During planning, teachers should complete this curriculum, so they have experienced this learning. process, and this ensures that the digital gap among staff is closed.
23 Teachers and students must have separate accounts for online communication.
24 Being a technology-based curriculum, rapid development and advances should be unpacked.
25 There generally two broad styles of programming block and text based coding.
26 Africa code week takes place on the African continent spear headed by business applications company, SAP. This initiative boasts African youth empowerment and is aligned to the United Nations (UN) Sustainable Development Goals.
27 https://hourofcode.com/
28 Algorithms were invented by Ebu Abdullah Muhammed Ibn Musa el Harezmi who is a Muslim mathematician.
29 Originally three laws were mentioned and years later the fourth law was added.
30 Citizenship was granted by Saudi Arabia: https://www.dw.com/en/saudi-arabia-grants-citizenship-to-robot-sophia/a-41150856
31 Deep learning is a subset of machine learning (ML) that is associated with artificial intelligence (AI). Deep learning or deep neural network, consists of networks that are capable of learning unsupervised and unstructured data.

32 Read more at: https://timesofindia.indiatimes.com/india/as-teachers-watch-robots-impart-lessons-in-this-school/articleshow/70867286.cms?utm_source=contentofinterest&utm_medium=text&utm_campaign=cppst
33 Online shopping website.
34 Promotes a greener environment and happy polar bears. Read more at: https://www.worldwildlife.org/pages/polar-bears-and-climate-change
35 These software programs can be available on Windows or Mac, and generates a virtual environment that simulates the movement of a robot.
36 Promoting kinesthetic learning environments.
37 The liberality of Freire's educational principle.

References

Abrahm, P. M., & Kenter, S. (1978). Tik-Tok and the three laws of robotics. *Science Fiction Studies, 5*(1), 67–80.

Ackermann, E. K. (2004). Constructing knowledge and transforming the world. In M. Tokoro & L. Steels (Eds.), *A learning zone of one's own: Sharing representations and flow in collaborative learning environments* (pp. 15–37). IOS Press.

Albertazzi, D., & Cobley, P. (2013). *The media: An introduction* (3rd ed.). Routledge.

Anistyasari, Y., & Kurniawan, A. (2018). Exploring computational thinking to improve energy-efficient programming skills. *MATEC Web of Conferences, 197*(2018), 1–4. https://doi.org/10.1051/matecconf/201819715011

Bates, A. W. (1988). Television, learning and distance education. *Journal of Educational Television, 14*(3), 213–225. https://doi.org/10.1080/0260741880140305

Brainerd, C. J. (2003). Jean Piaget: Learning, research, and American education. In B. J. Zimmerman & D. Schunk (Eds.), *Educational psychology: A century of contributions* (pp. 251–287). Lawrence Erlbaum Associates.

Buyukozturk, S., Cokluk, O., & Koklu, N. (2010). *The statistics for the social sciences* (6th ed.). Pegem Academy.

Coles, A. D. (1999). *Education week: Mass-produced pencil leaves its mark.* https://www.edweek.org/ew/articles/1999/06/16/40pencil.h18.html

Curzon, P. (2015). *Computational thinking: Searching to speak.* https://cs4fndownloads.files.wordpress.com/2016/02/searchingtospeak-booklet.pdf

D'Onfro, J. (2019). *Amazon's new delivery drone will start shipping packages in a matter of months.* https://www.forbes.com/sites/jilliandonfro/2019/06/05/amazon-new-delivery-drone-remars-warehouse-robots-alexa-prediction/#eoc08b1145f3

Denning, P. J. (2017). Remaining trouble spots with computational thinking. *Communications of the ACM, 60*(6), 33–39. https://doi.org/10.1145/2998438

Falloon, G. (2016). An analysis of young students' thinking when completing basic coding tasks using Scratch Jnr. on the iPad. *Journal of Computer Assisted Learning, 32*(6), 576–593. https://doi.org/10.1111/jcal.12155

Freire, P. (2018). *Pedagogy of the oppressed*. Bloomsbury Publishing.

Furner, J. M., & Kumar, D. D. (2007). The mathematics and science integration argument: A stand for teacher education. *Eurasia Journal of Mathematics, Science & Technology Education, 3*(3), 185–189. https://doi.org/10.12973/ejmste/75397

Gatouillat, A., Badr, Y., Massot, B., & Sejdić, E. (2018). Internet of medical things: A review of recent contributions dealing with cyber-physical systems in medicine. *IEEE Internet of Things Journal, 5*(5), 3810–3822. https://doi.org/ffi0.1109/JIOT.2018.2849014f

Gerlach, J. (2012). *STEM: Defying a simple definition*. http://www.nsta.org/publications/news/story.aspx?id=59305

Hannafin, M. J., & Hannafin, K. M. (2010). Cognition and student-centered, web-based learning: Issues and implications for research and theory. In M. Spector & D. Ifenthaler (Eds.), *Learning and instruction in the digital age* (pp. 11–23). Springer.

Heaney, L. (2019). Quantum computing and complexity in art. *Leonardo, 52*(3), 230–235. https://doi.org/10.1162/leon_a_01572

Hilty, E. B. (2018). *Thinking about schools: A foundations of education reader*. Routledge.

Jacob, S., Nguyen, H., Tofel-Grehl, C., Richardson, D., & Warschauer, M. (2018). Teaching computational thinking to English learners. *NYS TESOL Journal, 5*(2), 12–24.

Kalelioglu, F., Gulbahar, Y., & Kukul, V. (2016). A framework for computational thinking based on a systematic research review. *Baltic Journal of Modern Computing, 4*(3), 583–596.

Kalra, H. K., & Chadha, R. (2018). A review study on humanoid robot SOPHIA based on artificial intelligence. *International Journal of Technology and Computing, 4*(3), 31–33. https://doi.org/H10420688S219

Kim, B. H. (2016). Development of young children coding drone using block game. *Indian Journal of Science and Technology, 9*(44), 1–5.

Korkmaz, O., Cakir, R., Ozden, M. Y., Oluk, A., & Sarioglu, S. (2016). Investigation of individuals' computational thinking skills in terms of different variables. *Ondokuz Mayis University Journal of Faculty of Education, 34*(2), 68–87.

Li, S., Da Xu, L., & Zhao, S. (2018). 5G Internet of Things: A survey. *Journal of Industrial Information Integration, 10*(1), 1–9. https://doi.org/10.1016/j.jii.2018.01.005

Liu, B., & He, J. (2014, August 22–24). Teaching mode reform and exploration on the university computer basic based on computational thinking training in network environment. In *Proceedings of the 9th International Conference on Computer Science & Education* (pp. 59–62). https://doi.org/10.1109/ICCSE.2014.6926430

Luckin, R., Holmes, W., Griffiths, M., & Forcier, L. B. (2016). *Intelligence unleashed: An argument for AI in education*. Pearson Education.

Musson, A. E., & Robinson, E. (1959). The early growth of steam power. *The Economic History Review, 11*(3), 418–439. https://doi.org/10.1111/j.1468-0289.1959.tb01650.x

Muttappallymyalil, J., Mendis, S., John, L. J., Shanthakumari, N., Sreedharan, J., & Shaikh, R. B. (2016). Evolution of technology in teaching: Blackboard and beyond in medical education. *Nepal Journal of Epidemiology, 6*(3), 588. https://doi.org/10.3126/nje.v6i3.15870

Naidoo, J., & Govender, R. (2014). Exploring the use of a dynamic online software programme in the teaching and learning of trigonometric graphs. *Pythagoras, 35*(2), 45–57. https://doi.org/10.4102/pythagoras.v35i2.260

Naidoo, J., & Govender, R. (2019). Exploring in-service and pre-service teachers' perceptions of integrating technology-based tools when teaching circle geometry. *The International Journal of Science, Mathematics and Technology Learning, 26*(2), 29–49. https://doi.org/10.18848/2327-7971/CGP

Papert, S. (1980). *Mindstorms: Children, computers, and powerful ideas.* Harvester Press.

Philbeck, T., & Davis, N. (2019). The Fourth Industrial Revolution. *Journal of International Affairs, 72*(1), 17–22. https://doi.org/10.2307/26588339

Piaget, J. (1964). Development and learning. *Journal of Research in Science Teaching, 2*(1), 176–186.

Piaget, J. (1972). *The psychology of intelligence.* Littlefield.

Pierce, D., & Hathaway, A. (2018). The promise (and pitfalls) of AI for education: Artificial Intelligence could have a profound impact on learning, but it also raises key Questions. *The Journal (Technological Horizons in Education), 45*(3), 20.

Reynolds, R. (2011). Trends influencing the growth of digital textbooks in US higher education. *Publishing Research Quarterly, 27*(2), 178–187. https://doi.org/10.1007/s12109-011-9216-5

Romero, M., Lepage, A., & Lille, B. (2017). Computational thinking development through creative programming in higher education. *International Journal of Educational Technology in Higher Education, 14*(1), 42. https://doi.org/10.1186/s41239-017-0080-z

Roy, S., Williamson, C., & McLean, R. (2018). LMS performance issues: A case study of D2L. *ISCA Journal of Computers and Their Applications, 25*(3), 1–9.

Sano, A. (2019). *Newspaper economy: Coding will be mandatory in Japan's primary schools from 2020 Tokyo aims to plug IT worker shortage and catch up to other countries.* https://asia.nikkei.com/Economy/Coding-will-be-mandatory-in-Japan-s-primary-schools-from-2020

Schwab, K. (2016). *The Fourth Industrial Revolution.* World Economic Forum. https://www.weforum.org/agenda/2016/01/the-fourth-industrial-revolution-what-it-means-and-how-to-respond/

Shor, I., & Freire, P. (1987). *A pedagogy for liberation: Dialogues on transforming education.* Bergin & Garvey.

Skinner, B. F. (1958). Teaching machines. *Science, 128*(3330), 969–977. https://doi.org/10.1126/science.128.3330.969

SONA. (2019). *State of the Nation Address.* https://www.gov.za/speeches/president-cyril-ramaphosa-2019-state-nation-address

Ullas, S. (2019). *Lessons in this school.* http://timesofindia.indiatimes.com/articleshow/70867286.cms?utm_source=contentofinterest&utm_medium=text&utm_campaign=cppst

Voogt, J., Fisser, P., Good, J., Mishra, P., & Yadav, A. (2015). Computational thinking in compulsory education: Towards an agenda for research and practice. *Education and Information Technologies, 20*(4), 715–728. https://doi.org/10.1007/s10639-015-9412-6

Weller, C. (2017). *Meet the first-ever robot citizen: A humanoid named Sophia that once said it would 'destroy humans'.* https://www.businessinsider.com/meet-the-first-robot-citizen-sophia-animatronic-humanoid-2017-10

Wing, J. (2006). Computational thinking. *Communications of the ACM, 49*(3), 33–35. https://doi.org/0001-0782/06/0300

PART 2

The 21st-Century Classroom Environment

CHAPTER 4

Visualizing as a Means of Understanding in the Fourth Industrial Revolution Environment

Vimolan Mudaly

Abstract

Visualization has been a subject of much research, and recently, technology in terms of the Fourth Industrial Revolution movement has also been in vogue. While visualization serves as a strong tool for problem-solving, technology offers learners the possibility of experiencing mathematics and science in a dynamic environment, with diagrams changing by simply dragging or implementing a code. If these changes are visible and understandable, then they offer opportunities for an increased conviction that something is either true or not. This interpretivist qualitative study combined these areas of study to explore the possibility of engaging learners using technology from a visual perspective. Thirteen in-service teachers were asked to design lessons that incorporated visuals and learners were allowed to engage in these lessons actively. These participants then became co-researchers of the study. The research sites varied, and therefore the lessons planned and delivered were not the same for all participants. The participants reported an increase in learner confidence and a subsequent improvement in understanding of concepts. The framework that was used as a lens to look at the data was the Iterative Visualization Cycle, which was an adaptation of Kolb's Experiential Learning Theory. Much of what is written is from the participants' perspectives because it was their voices that needed to be highlighted.

1 Introduction

Krantz (2015) stated that "never mind the shame that in the past, we were not concerned about teaching [mathematics]. Now we are all concerned, and that is good" (p. xi). The concern arose out of the prevailing evidence that learners are underperforming in tests and examinations. Research has shown that teachers are not doing well in their teaching. Naidoo (2005, p. 198) found that:

the practices in these teachers' classrooms, there was a tendency towards regimentation in the learning environment, with the teacher clearly in authority. Classroom interactions were dominated by a focus on getting the right answers, usually through some procedure given by the teacher. When pupils were left to work on exercises themselves, they did this largely in silence. The weaving of fundamental pedagogics into the social fabric of these classroom practices is highly visible.

But, in reforming teaching we are beginning to engage our learners actively through using technology and skills that require the use of visuals, both physically and mentally. The critical goal of teacher education is classroom success for the learner. Hence, teacher preparation must involve ideas that extend their teaching methodologies to reach far beyond the traditional chalk and talk.

My experiences as a teacher educator and researcher show that in preparing participants for the task of teaching mathematics, they struggle with the different approaches available to them. The traditional teaching method is useful but is becoming archaic as we move into the 21st century. Shulman (1987, p. 13) claimed that teaching began with an act of reason, continued with the process of reasoning, culminating in performances of imparting, eliciting, involving, or enticing. He further stated that after a period of reflection, the process repeats itself. He highlighted teaching as the processes of comprehension and reasoning and, as transformation and reflection (1987, p. 13).

The ideas of Shulman (1986, 1987) combined with Kolb's Experiential Learning Theory (1984) provide an ideal framework with which to examine preservice teacher development. Shulman specifically referred to the action of teaching, while Kolb's theory refers to the process of learning. This combination is ideal for exploring the learning the preservice teachers experience as they develop the skills to become proficient in their field. The model illustrated in Figure 4.1 combines the two theories but from a visual perspective.

2 Future of Mathematics Education

Zinger, Tate, and Warschauer (2017, p. 579) noted: "that positive participant outcomes have been achieved when teachers are provided with technical support and professional development for the integration of technology in the classroom". That is exactly where the future of education should be heading. The advent of Covid-19 suddenly thrust the world into a frenzy looking for technological solutions for remote teaching. Teachers are currently not prepared for the use of alternative methods.

But, creating deep conceptual understanding in learners is an important role of teachers. The expansion of mathematical knowledge involves the process of creating new knowledge by forming associations with new information and previously acquired knowledge. Generally, learners fail to see these links and hence they become conceptually deficient. The understanding of mathematical concepts is enhanced by the integration of computer technology into the classroom teaching and learning strategy. Technology, in particular virtual manipulatives, is significant in the way it influences conceptual development in mathematics learning. These virtual manipulatives, including Computer Generated Animations, GeoGebra, Sketchpad or any other dynamic software tool, could mediate the learning of mathematical concepts as we teach in the era of the Fourth Industrial Revolution (4IR). Also, with the advent of easier computing facilities and smartphones, children have greater access to learning using an array of technology. This then provides a new dimension to learning. According to Martínez, Bárcena and Rodríguez (2005, p. 1):

> …true understanding of mathematics takes place as learners progress through phases of action (physical and mental), abstraction (the process by which actions become mentally entrenched so that learners can reflect and act on them), and reflection (deliberate analysis of one's thinking). Moving through these phases time after time enables learners to construct increasingly sophisticated mental models of the abstraction.

3   Use of Technology

This study aimed to explore whether technological manipulatives could provide learners with the necessary tools to enable them to understand mathematical concepts through their engagement with them. The dominance of technology in almost all spheres of human life and the highly digitized world has created a paradigm shift in the way we look at teaching and learning in the era of the 4IR. The idea that the teacher is the sage on the stage, wielding a stick of chalk as s/he approaches the board is now an archaic one. Teaching and learning have expanded to include a variety of media, including computers, radio, television, podcasts or Internet. We must be acutely conscious of the fact that technology also includes non-electronic media and tools (paper cuttings, bending of wires to form parallelograms, and so on). Technology refers to all the tools or paraphernalia that learners use in their quest to establish a deep understanding of an unknown phenomenon.

But dynamic electronic technology has a distinct advantage in that it allows the learner to engage in more experiences in a shorter period of time. According to the National Council of Teachers of Mathematics (2000, p. 24):

> …electronic technologies…furnish visual images of mathematical ideas, they facilitate organizing and analyzing data, and they compute efficiently and accurately. They can support investigations by learners in every area of mathematics. When technology tools are available, learners can focus on decision making, reflection, reasoning, and problem-solving.

4 Visualization

The influence of technology is significant, but its value in mathematics is measured in how technology can be used to create a scaffold between the previous knowledge and new concepts to be taught. While the 4IR has created a digital miasma (a large portion of the world is being left behind), its value will be felt in the way it is utilized to reinforce ideas that may be too abstract for children to grasp. That is why Arcavi's (2003, p. 217) definition of visualization is so significant. His often-quoted definition captured the essence of visualization when he stated that:

> Visualization is the ability, the process and the product of creation, interpretation, use of and reflection upon pictures, images, diagrams, in our minds, on paper or with technological tools, with the purpose of depicting and communicating information, thinking about and developing previously unknown ideas and advancing understandings. (Arcavi, 2003, p. 217)

The principle of the definition lies in the notion that ideas can be created by reflecting on pictures, diagrams or images, whether they are on paper or through the use of technology. This is about physically seeing and then mentally reflecting on what is seen. This definition captures the essential link between visualization and methodologies that need to be employed in the 21st century. It is not only about the influx of new and complex technology. It must also include the different ways in which new and existing technologies and methodologies can be adapted to cater for learners in this fast-changing digital scenario.

5 Theoretical and Conceptual Framework

Figure 4.1 describes the process of learning through experiences that applies to all learning but was used for the analysis of data collected from preservice teachers. The process begins with active engagement. This could be a physical activity (for example, drawing, reading, listening or the use of technology) or a mental activity (for example, imagining, recalling). The physical activity relates to the senses, mainly sight and the mental activity relates mainly to insight. In this stage, the learner does something to the information available – either physically or mentally. This is the doing stage. But the process of meaning-making may require more than one attempt. Often it involves an iteration between internalization and externalization processes. The learner acts on the information physically, a level of understanding results by associating the new information with previously acquired knowledge and then the learner returns to the activity.

This process of 'acting' on the information ('doing') and then reflecting ('thinking') on it can result in an iterative process of doing and thinking. These mental and physical manipulations are often subtle and occur almost simultaneously. These may be accompanied by mental images and physical images (technology, diagrams, pictures and sketches). This is the stage where insight develops ('I see'). The use of visuals, technology and dynamic software enables

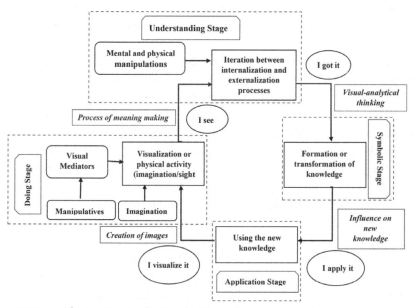

FIGURE 4.1   The iterative visualization thinking cycle

the learner to work with a visual, analyze its properties and establish a level of understanding. With the new understanding, further analysis ensues to establish a higher level of understanding. This visual-analytical thinking will continue until the requisite level of understanding is attained ('I got it'). This is the symbolic stage where understanding results in the formation of new knowledge and the transformation of existing knowledge. At this step, the learner should be able to produce a proof. The final stage is the application stage where the new knowledge is used to explain and solve problems in the contexts presented. Once attained, the process may begin with a new concept.

The visual mediators may be diagrams, pictures or dynamic computer-generated diagrams that can stimulate the learner into thinking about a specific concept or idea. For example, a picture of a triangle may elicit thoughts about the sizes of angles and sides, the sum of the angles, the side opposite the largest angle is the largest, or the area of the triangle using a formula. A picture tends to draw on previously acquired knowledge (a priori). If the knowledge is well understood then easy recall of relationships is possible. Using imagination or mental pictures is similar but slightly more difficult. For example, if I asked learners to recall a rhombus, learners may picture different types of rhombi but the properties will be similar. These mental images will depend on the previous experiences of the learner. It would be impossible for the learner to mentally picture a rhombus if s/he had never seen one before. Both physical and mental images could be powerful tools. Similarly, in the understanding stage, the manipulation of these images is crucial for deep conceptual understanding.

An additional model that is crucial in understanding the iterative processes involved was presented by Chaouki and Hasenbank (2013) (Figure 4.2). The model explains the conceptual and procedural understanding of the acquisition of knowledge in a succinct way. The model carefully elucidates the relationships between shallow and deep understanding of concepts. They illustrate the acquisition of both procedural and conceptual knowledge by using a three-dimensional figure, which measures conceptual understanding against the skills acquired by participants who are novices at solving problems, and compares these with those of the more experienced, as the participant improves at solving the problems. The model illustrates the types of understanding achieved as a learner goes from being a novice to becoming experienced and efficient at working with the mathematics concepts.

Novice learners' conceptual understanding is shallow with little connection between the new concept and previous concepts. Often the procedures involved are not understood or memorized and it appears as if the brain has become overloaded with new facts. As understanding deepens, they begin to form connections between new and prior concepts, but understanding is still illusory. Although procedures are executed slowly they are still not well-understood. Even the 'practiced' can also have a shallow understanding of mathematical concepts. In this case, procedures are performed by rote, and although concepts are well-memorized, they are still disconnected from other related concepts. If deep understanding is to be achieved by the 'practiced' or experienced learner, then procedures ought to be executed intelligently with understanding and new concepts become well connected with all previous but related concepts.

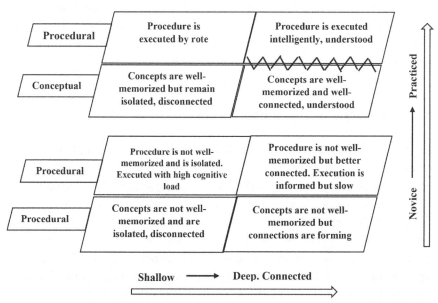

FIGURE 4.2   Improving understanding in Algebra 1: A deeper understanding of Algebra/Math (adapted from Chaouki & Hasenbank, 2013)

6   Methodology

As part of their independent research task in one of their Honors modules (Curriculum Development in Science and Mathematics Education), participants were asked to prepare lessons that specifically used visualization as a strategy to teach concepts in mathematics and science. The participants were encouraged to use a variety of computer software, videos and demonstrations so that the visualizations became dynamic and, in some instances, dynamic. This was a qualitative study located within the interpretivist paradigm. The aim was to try to develop a deeper understanding of how these strategies employed in classrooms would influence learner meaning-making. Although there were 49 participants in the class, participation in the research itself was completely voluntary and 13 participants chose to become co-researchers.

The planning of their lessons, choice of topics and methods used were all left entirely to them. The only stipulation was that they had to conduct three to five lessons using the chosen methodology in one week and record their experiences. Being novices at research, the participants were tentative with what they reported but there was sufficient information to report on their research findings. After the participants had completed their lessons they were asked to complete a questionnaire using Google Forms and were interviewed in a group using Zoom. The location of the schools varied from urban to rural areas in KwaZulu-Natal, and the facilities available in each school ranged from fully equipped with technology to those schools which had none.

7   Findings, Analysis and Discussion

Participants used both visual (drawings, sketches and mental pictures) and physical activities in their co-research activities. They were then asked to comment on what they learned from the exercise of engaging in these visualization activities. Participant S1 stated that his learners had to also use both physical objects (including computer-generated diagrams) and their imagination (mental). His learners were asked to firstly visualize a 3-D object to calculate its area and were then shown a computer demonstration of a rotating object to see how their mental images compared with what they had imagined. Learners were expected to compare the calculations in both instances.

S2, on the other hand, enticed his learners into drawing diagrams by listening to the statement of a theorem. They were then guided through a GeoGebra discovery session. This involved a combination of visuals that they saw and the visuals that they had to imagine. Participant S4 used computer simulations in his lessons. They were able to see, through the simulations, how the science experiments worked, and then, they were able to carry out similar experiments on their own. According to participant S4 the learners:

> did, in some sense, use imagination to translate the simulation into real-life situations in the applications as well. (Questionnaire, 25 February 2020)

A number of participants simply used physical diagrams which they asked learners to interpret, manipulate or use together with words to understand a concept. Participant S7 did suggest though that using visuals mentally and physically removed some of the language barriers that are common in South African classrooms. Participant S12, who also used Sketchpad demonstrations, stated that he:

> learnt that a visualization is a motivational tool that enhanced the teaching and learning environment of my classroom. While working with the assessment task I observed that visualization helped learners understand and grasp the mathematical concepts easily. The use of visualization simplified the concepts in such a way that learners no longer saw transformations as abstract. (Questionnaire, 25 February 2020)

The thematic analysis was determined by the general responses of the participants in the online questionnaire and from the Zoom interview. Similar responses were clustered into categories and arguments evolved around these participant responses.

7.1 Learners' Manipulation of the Figure in the Task

The participants were asked to comment on their learners' ability to manipulate the diagrams, figures and software and, the level of understanding the activity generated. Participant S1 felt the learners were able to easily manipulate the figures both physically and mentally. As is evident in the extract from the Focus Group Interview that follows:

> Yes, they did, they were then able to use their visual reasoning even after the figures were manipulated, where they were asked to imagine if the 3-D objects were either open or closed or if other parts were removed. Making a connection between what they had seen and what they were asked, made it easy for learners to answer the questions correctly. (Focus group interview, 25 February 2020)

There was consensus among the participants that learners were able to manipulate the diagrams, figures and software. In this process of meaning-making, the learners were able to utilize the given artefacts to develop a greater sense of the concept itself, resulting in more in-depth understanding. Jiang et al. (2011, p. 4) also concur that that to manipulate a diagram, "techniques based on an underlying structure of the diagram are effective and efficient". They worked on hand-drawn diagrams but this could easily be extrapolated to other diagrams as well. Participant S7, who also worked with 3-D shapes, found that:

the learners who were exposed to the computer-generated 3-D shapes could easily calculate areas even without having the shapes in front of them. They were able to create mental images and perform their calculations with ease. These learners seemed to have a greater understanding of working with 3D shapes. They understood how to find the surface area and the volume of the given images. (Questionnaire, 25 February 2020)

Participant S4 found that the learners understood the activity as well as the PHET (Physics Education Technology) simulation. He stated that:

they got a visual interpretation and understanding of the phenomena first and this created the knowledge for them that they may have found hard to understand through ordinary, plain text. They did ask questions; however, most of these were trivial as they developed their own understandings. (Focus group interview, 25 February 2020)

Many of the participants reported that the diagrams and visuals used were self-explanatory, and the learners required little guidance. There may have been instances where the participant (as the teacher) was called upon to explain, but in general, the diagrams or activities were self-explanatory. Participant S2 chose to work with two theorems in Euclidean geometry. He decided to use GeoGebra to demonstrate these theorems diagrammatically. Learners had to measure lengths and angles so that they could draw hypotheses about the relationships between the different angles and lengths. This was experiential and would have involved both mental and physical manipulations.

7.2 *Learners' Reaction to the Activity*

The participants were asked about the learners' reaction to the activity and how they responded. There was a great deal of enthusiasm exhibited by the learners and an unusual willingness to participate in the activities. This could have been as a result of the uniqueness of the tasks, but nonetheless, they did engage more than expected. Participant S13 observed that:

while learners were answering their activity, some learners were moving their hands like we discussed earlier in the lesson for the different types of transformation. Additionally, some learners wrote the lyrics of the song on a page to help them recall transformation. I noticed that learners were excited to move their hands to show the transformation. However, when the learners watched the video of transformation, they were very enthusiastic and asked to watch it more than once. (Focus group interview, 25 February 2020)

Participant S1 felt that the learners understood and answered the questions about nets of the 3-D objects with relative ease. More importantly, though, was their ability to connect what they were learning with their previous knowledge. In some instances, participants used pencil and paper methods first and then other visual strategies, including computer software. Participant S2, for example, tried to teach participants two theorems using 'chalk and talk'. Most participants could not understand, nor could they recall even the statement of the theorem. But when they were exposed to GeoGebra:

> they were quick to arrive at the conclusion of both the theorem and its converse. (Focus group interview, 25 February 2020)

There was also an overall tendency for learners to want to work together. Participant S11 observed that the learners tried to add to the activity by providing their own interpretations of what they saw and also helped other learners understand. Participation was not normal in her classes because of learners' fear of not understanding and 'looking silly' in front of the entire class. According to participant S11, the learners' initial reaction was that it looked easy and simple to comprehend as they could 'see' it with their own eyes. Philominraj, Jeyabalan and Vidal-Silva (2017, p. 54) also concluded from their research that "when learners are introduced into the world of images, spontaneous creativity towards the goal is achieved". In the current research, it could have been the activities, but there seemed to have been an overwhelming acceptance of the ideas around the visual strategies. Technology makes the creation and manipulation of these diagrams much easier.

7.3 *Learners' Ability to Engage with Concepts*

There was sufficient evidence to demonstrate that the visualization of the lessons enabled the learners to engage actively in the lessons and with the concepts under scrutiny. For example, participant S1 felt that the learners:

> were able to picture the 3-D objects and connect them with the previous lesson on calculating the area of a 2-D shape to enhance their understanding. Pictures and diagrams helped them to quickly connect concepts as they showed understanding. (Questionnaire, 25 February 2020)

To see learners develop this relationship with current and previous work while working within the domain of visualization, was not unusual. For the process of meaning-making to occur and the concepts to be well-connected, being able to see the relationship as a visual proof often plays a more profound role than simply being told about the relationship. In a similar way, participant

S2 discovered that by becoming engrossed in the GeoGebra activity the learners were able, on their own, to calculate missing lengths on the circles or triangles given to them. The fact that they engaged in the activity and arrived at the hypothesis themselves contributed to their confidence and success at solving the problems. Participant S12 also found that:

> they were able to integrate the activity with the concept because it was their findings that allowed them to draw a conjecture, and generalize and that was, in fact, the theorem. (Focus group interview, 25 February 2020)

Other patterns also emerged. Participant S8 wrote about the procedure that her learners followed after observing them work through a few examples. These were her observations during geometry lessons. The learners would read the questions, pause and read the questions again. They would then underline or highlight important words or known facts. This was either followed by the learner drawing a diagram or adding some information onto a given diagram. Generally, learners tried to include what is given in the statements onto the diagram. The learners would then try to solve the problem on the diagram itself. This is a fairly significant observation because it shows the role that the visuals play in both understanding the concept and in the application of the concept.

This type of visualization did not have to necessarily occur in complex problems only. Participant S4 worked with probability, specifically on the use of Venn-diagrams and the use of shading to show the union of sets, complement, universal set and that which was mutually exclusive. She found that the learners were able to transfer the meaning of the shading of the various diagrams to the written work and find the solutions of the questions in the activities given.

7.4 *Learners' Iteration between the Activity and the Question*

Learners' ability to engage with concepts may require them to iterate between the question and the activity several times. As was observed by participant S8, there was a general tendency of the learners to read their questions several times as they solved the problem. The participants could not explain the phenomenon because they felt that if the learners understood the question once, then there was no need to revert to the question again. Participant S1's observation showed that the learners read the question a few times then sketched a diagram and then returned to the question to see whether the diagram made 'sense'. This is indeed a significant step because the sense-making process requires that the learner attempts to create a deeper understanding of the problem itself before proceeding with the solution.

7.5 *Participant Observations*

As co-researchers, it was important to understand what the Participants observed as they watched their learners work through the different activities. These observations were significant in locating the role visualization played in conceptual understanding. Participant S1 acknowledged that visual representations helped the learners understand the questions and what the question expects of them. The diagrams and pictures themselves assist learners to visualize the different parts of the question and then they draw the diagram. They then answer the question based on the drawn diagram while making connections with previously learned knowledge.

Many of the participants observed the learners work both individually and collectively. If a visual was not providing sufficient information for some then other learners would become actively involved in explaining and sharing ideas. This participatory learning style was encouraged throughout the research among all participant researchers. It was observed that the learners who had knowledge, helped and shared what they understood with others. Some of the participants observed that the learners showed greater enthusiasm in class with unusual concentration levels. This was not a longitudinal study so it cannot be stated with absolute confidence that it was the visualization activities that created these changes in the learners.

Participant S2 also made an encouraging observation. He found that hardly any of the learners had developed serious misconceptions. They were applying what was learnt in the activity appropriately and it seemed as if the fact that they could see many of the concepts depicted in diagrams or using GeoGebra helped eradicate possible misconceptions.

7.6 *The Role the Visuals Played in Understanding of the Concepts*

There was an overwhelming consensus that without the visuals the learners would have struggled to understand the concepts. Cook (2012), while specifically writing about science, stated that most often, visuals are used to depict phenomena and relationships that students cannot observe or experience directly and this seems to be true for mathematics as well. The participants felt that it was better when the learners worked with what they could see. This was reinforced by participant S2 when he said that the visuals allowed them to see what they were learning. He was convinced that:

> Seeing is believing – and in this sense, learners were not learning through text which makes concepts abstract. They were also able to interact with the visualization tools and better comprehend the concepts. (Focus group interview, 25 February 2020)

Some comparison was also drawn to previous experiences of the learners. Participant S3 claimed that previously learners were not adept with solving geometric riders since they began working with visualization strategies; they are more willing to tackle these problems. In measuring the actual success of her learners, participant S8 indicated that more than 75% of the class managed to pass with more than 60% accuracy. This was not the norm in her class. Generally, less than 40% of the learners passed with a mark of 40% or more. She also asked her learners to complete an evaluation form, and their responses generally indicated that learning with visuals deepened their understanding and even suggested that this type of teaching also be adapted to other topics. Participant S9 captured a significant role that visuals played in the understanding of concepts. He found that the visual used:

> played an important role by condensing a large amount of data into one diagram and this made it easier for the learner to make sense of it. (Questionnaire, 25 February 2020)

He went on to add that these visuals provided an accessible way to see and understand trends and patterns (Questionnaire, 25 February 2020).

The participants were convinced that the visuals were critical for deep conceptual understanding. Participant S1 stated that after the use of visual representations, learners used different methods to solve problems and found that all the strategies provided the same correct answer. Similarly, participant S2 found that learners showed a great deal of understanding in the review session at the end of the lesson. Learners showed confidence and voluntarily answered questions. Other participants found that the learners were now able to work independently or in groups and at their own pace. They were not scared to tackle unfamiliar problems using visualization.

Cook (2012) was fairly specific and stated that visuals are common in textbooks, in presentations developed by teachers and learners, and computer-based software. He further argued that when keeping diagrams simple and explanations short, teachers must monitor student learning to ensure alternate conceptions do not result (p. 67). This resonates well with the findings of this research.

7.7 *Visualization and Its Contribution to New Knowledge*

The experiences of the participants indicated that the learners had developed useful knowledge. Participant S1 felt that the learners:

> were able to use their imagination to understand the question. Connecting what they learned with real-life experiences to answer the questions.

Even in their responses, they made use of diagrams as scaffolds towards reaching the correct answer. (Focus group interview, 25 February 2020)

There were other positive observations made by the participants regarding the learners' renewed commitment to working with problems. Participant S3 was convinced that new knowledge was indeed created, and it was this knowledge that provided the learners with the confidence to solve and apply theorems and riders. Participant S7 found that her learners understood the difference between 2-D and 3-D objects and could calculate areas and volumes quite easily. There were other obvious observations such as the learners understood a specific section such as the Midpoint Theorem. There was also related knowledge acquired using the different instruments, technology and software. The knowledge that the learners gained went beyond just the theorems and axioms in the curriculum. Participant S13 stated that:

> prior to the use of visualizations, learners struggled to understand the concepts of transformation and they were unable to make correlations with the concepts to everyday life. However, once the learners completed the activity using a yellow arrow and their hands the meaning of rotation, reflection and translation became apparent. I found that learners were able to give me examples of where we see this in everyday life. They were able to give me an example of reflection as a mirror and that the wheel of the bus and car rotates without me giving examples. (Focus group interview, 25 February 2020)

In most cases, the learners showed great improvement in their ability to answer questions in the specific sections. They were able to apply the knowledge learned and showed a greater tendency to use diagrams. Even when they were expected to calculate the surface area of simple figures, they chose to draw a diagram to get to the answer. Many used visual reasoning first and then reverted to a written solution. The participants who used technology in their classrooms found that learners grasped the concepts quicker and with greater ease because

> they saw more examples in a shorter space of time. (Questionnaire, 25 February 2020)

With the use of technology:

> they were able to find the generalization themselves, then they were able to state the theorem, and apply it. (Questionnaire, 25 February 2020)

Yusoff, Katmon, Ahmad and Miswan (2013) acknowledged that visualization of knowledge is widely used in the education field for knowledge transfer and creation. The data evidence in this research corroborates their findings and it shows how technology can be used quite easily to develop new knowledge, by visualizing previous and current knowledge.

8 Conclusion

The visual task on its own was not enough. Learners had to engage with the visual manipulative, reflect on it sufficiently and create their own understanding. In many of the cases the learners were given opportunities to mentally or physically manipulate the diagrams so that what they saw or imagined could fit into the schema of understanding already established. The learners who worked with the 3-D figures, for example, used the 2-D knowledge quite well and their imagined figures to complete the tasks. The computer-generated shapes provided adequate links to their *a priori* knowledge so that they could easily find ways of determining the areas of the given shapes. There were many instances where the learners used the reflective process to iterate between the physical shapes and the imagined shapes, and even manipulated then mentally. The learners who worked with transformations were able to recall what they had seen in the video presentation and then use their hands to recall the movements. But seeing the changes effected on the computer-enabled the learners to draw quick conclusions.

Those learners who worked with GeoGebra verified the truth of the result very quickly and were able to state what they saw as the relationship. This is the power of using visualization in the context of technology. It enables the learner to actively engage with the artefacts and develop an increased level of conviction through a rapid and responsive meaning-making activity. It is the 'seeing' combined with the available evidence that convinces the learners that what they are experiencing is true. This ensures that concepts become well-connected and well-memorized. Palais (1999, p. 648) who worked extensively with technology stated that "applied mathematicians find that the highly interactive nature of the images produced by recent mathematical visualization software allows them to do mathematical experiments with an ease never before possible". It creates ease of use and allows for ease in understanding.

Visualization using technology in the 21st century in the era of the 4IR as a strategic methodology has distinct advantages for learners who struggle to see the abstractness of mathematics and science. Learning opportunities must be provided in ways that are accessible, understandable and meaningful to our struggling learners. Becoming more visually connected in a classroom may be the solution.

References

Arcavi, A. (2003). The role of visual representations in the learning of mathematics. *Educational Studies in Mathematics, 52*, 215–241.

Chaouki, R., & Hasenbank, J. F. (2013). *Improving understanding in Algebra 1: A deeper understanding of Algebra/Math*. Retrieved June 13, 2016, from http://www.slideserve.com/elina/adeeper-understanding-of-algebra-1188586

Cook, M. (2012). Teaching with visuals in a science classroom. *Science Scope, 64*–67.

Jiang, Y., Tian, F., Zhang, X., Dai, G., & Wang, H. (2011). Understanding, manipulating and searching hand-drawn concept maps. ACM Transactions on Intelligent Systems and Technology, 3(1). doi:10.1145/2036264.2036275

Kolb, D. A. (1984). *Experiential learning: Experience as the source of learning and development*. Prentice-Hall.

Krantz, S. G. (2015). *How to teach mathematics* (3rd ed.). American Mathematics Society.

Martinez, M., Barcena, F., & Rodriguez, S. (2005). *ICT in mathematics education: Geometry problem solving with applets. Recent research developments in learning technologies*. Paper presented at the 3rd International Conference on Multimedia and Information and Communication Technologies, Caceres, Spain.

Naidoo, A. (2005). Pre-service mathematics teacher education: Building a future on the legacy of apartheid's colleges of education. In R. Vithal, J. Adler, & C. Keitel (Eds.), *Researching mathematics education in South Africa: Perspectives, practices and possibilities*. HSRC Press.

National Council of Teachers of Mathematics. (2000). *Principles and standards for school mathematics*. National Council of Teachers of Mathematics.

Palais, R. S. (1999). The visualization of mathematics: Towards a mathematical exploratorium. *Notices of the AMS, 46*(6), 647–658.

Philominraj, A., Jeyabalan, D., & Vidal-Silva, C. (2017). Visual learning: A learner-centred approach to enhance English language teaching. *English Language Teaching, 10*(3), 54–62.

Presmeg, N. C. (1992). Prototypes, metaphors, metonymies and imaginative rationality in high school mathematics. *Educational Studies in Mathematics, 23*, 595–610.

Shulman, L. S. (1986). Those who understand: Knowledge growth in teaching. *Educational Researcher, 15*(2), 4–14.

Shulman, L. S. (1987). Knowledge and teaching: Foundations of the new reform. *Harvard Educational Review, 57*(1), 1–22.

Stylianou, D. A., & Silver, E. A. (2004). The role of visual representations in advanced mathematical problem solving: An examination of expert-novice similarities and differences. *Mathematical Thinking and Learning, 6*(4), 353–387.

Yusoff, Z., Katmon, S. A., Ahmad, M. Z., & Miswan, S. H. M. (2013, September). *Visual representation: Enhancing students' learning engagement through knowledge visualization*. Paper presented at the International Conference on Informatics and Creative Multimedia. https://www.researchgate.net/publication/261226062

Zinger, D., Tate, T., & Warschauer, M. (2017). Learning and teaching with technology: Technological pedagogy and teacher practice. In D. J. Clandinin & J. Husu (Eds.), *The Sage handbook of research on teacher education* (pp. 577–593). Sage.

CHAPTER 5

Transforming the Classroom Context: Mathematics Teachers' Experiences of the Use of Technology-Enabled Pedagogy for Embracing the Fourth Industrial Revolution

Jayaluxmi Naidoo

Abstract

Embracing the Fourth Industrial Revolution within education contexts is an important issue being researched globally. Within mathematics education contexts, coupled with embracing the Fourth Industrial Revolution are issues of what it means to teach within the 21st-century classroom. This chapter draws attention to a study that explored mathematics teachers and lecturers experiences of using technology-enabled pedagogy for the 21st-century classroom. This qualitative, interpretive study was located at one university within KwaZulu-Natal, South Africa. The study was framed within the ambits of connectivism. Participants were invited to an interactive workshop focusing on the use of technology-enabled pedagogy for the 21st-century classroom. Subsequently, participants were interviewed based on their experiences of the use of technology-enabled pedagogic strategies. The findings of this study exhibit that participants were empowered to transform their traditional pedagogy to embrace the Fourth Industrial Revolution. Furthermore, the findings of this study indicate that participants were willing to transform their existing pedagogy to cater to the 21st-century classroom context founded on the needs and learning styles of their students. Two main themes surfaced from this study: Limitations and strengths of using technology-enabled pedagogy. After the data coding, subthemes emerged. These themes and subthemes are discussed in detail in this chapter. Globally, these findings have relevance when considering the role of the Fourth Industrial Revolution within educational contexts.

1 Introduction

As we teach within the era of the Fourth Industrial Revolution (4IR), there are various debates on how existing classroom contexts ought to be transformed to cater to technology-enabled learning. Technology-enabled learning refers to the effective integration of technology-based tools within classroom contexts to facilitate students' learning (Ertmer & Ottenbreit-Leftwich, 2012). Teachers[1] ought to be sufficiently trained for preparing learners[2] with the 21st-century skills that are necessary to address the strengths and challenges linked with embracing the Fourth Industrial Revolution. However, if there is an imbalance between the curricula, transforming the classroom[3] context and professional development for teachers, then neither teachers nor students will be 4IR ready.

This chapter reports on a study which sought to explore mathematics teachers' experiences on the use of technology-enabled pedagogy for transforming their classroom context.

2   Literature Review

2.1   *Exploring the 21st-Century Classroom Context*

The capacity and technology that is required for creating digital learning environments extend far beyond the traditional classroom (Boothe & Clark, 2014). Technology in the 21st-century classroom serves as an essential tool to enhance the digital learning environment (Boholano, 2017). Digital learning environments support the effective integration of digital tools (for example, computers and mobile devices) to enable pedagogy (Buzzard, Crittenden, Crittenden, & McCarty, 2011).

Also, the physical space within the classroom needs to be considered to ensure that technology-enabled pedagogy is sustained and effective (Clemmons, 2013). Within the traditional classroom context, learners are situated at desks surrounding one another; however, within the 21st-century classroom context, global real-time collaboration through the use of digital tools are enabled. This means that learners do not need to be at the same place or be present at the same time for teaching and learning to take place.

The 21st-century classroom supports pedagogy which encourages critical thinking, hands-on learning, collaboration, problem-solving approaches, inquiry-based teaching and learning, the use of digital tools and technology-enabled pedagogy (Goertz, 2015). Also, notions of the 21st-century classroom advocate for the teacher to assume the role of a facilitator within the classroom context (Boothe & Clark, 2014). Teachers are also required to ensure that students have the necessary skills that are essential to embrace learning within the era of the Fourth Industrial Revolution. These skills include the ability to construct new ideas, assess and analyze the information offered, collaborate to create different problem-solving approaches and use inquiry-based learning to apply their understandings to their previous educational experiences (Boholano, 2017).

To assist teachers in ensuring that they enhance their existing pedagogy to teach effectively within the 21st-century classroom, teachers require professional development focusing on this area. Along similar lines, Borko (2004) and Darling-Hammond (2017) argue that teachers' professional development is essential for transforming the classroom context, ensuring effective teaching and improving students' learning outcomes.

2.2 Using Technology-Enabled Pedagogy to Embrace the Fourth Industrial Revolution

Since the arrival of the Fourth Industrial Revolution has been acknowledged by Klaus Schwab and the World Economic Forum, there has been much debate about it. The Fourth Industrial Revolution (4IR) is a technological revolution that has transformed our way of life (Schwab, 2016). The 4IR is described as the merging of the physical world and the virtual world, creating a more globally connected society. The 4IR guides the role of Higher Education institutions to prepare students for the digital era by incorporating the use of technology within revised curricula.

Technology has always been a part of the teaching and learning environment and has been used to facilitate students' learning. However, it is essential to consider that technology has transformed dramatically with time. Moreover, accessibility to a variety of digital tools has amplified the use of technology-enabled pedagogy (Buzzard, Crittenden, Crittenden, & McCarty, 2011). With technology being a part of our daily life, it is essential to rethink the concept of integrating technology within pedagogy. The aim of this integration ought to support the learning process.

Thus, learning with technology has become essential for the 21st-century classroom. This means that technology-enabled pedagogy ought to become a fundamental part of the learning experience and a necessary consideration for teachers within the 21st-century classroom context. Teachers may adopt a blended teaching and learning approach, whereby teaching shifts from the traditional 'chalk and talk' pedagogy to incorporate the use of technology-enabled pedagogy. This type of pedagogy aims to introduce a combination of online educational resources and opportunities for online interaction, together with traditional classroom methods (Lalima & Dangwal, 2017).

Presently, technology is regarded as being distinct from teaching and learning, and professional development workshops generally describe how to use technology but not necessarily how to embed technology effectively within classrooms. Similarly, Ertmer and Ottenbreit-Leftwich (2012) maintain that teacher professional development workshops for technology integration generally focus on administration rather than how technology may be used effectively for instruction. This implies that at present, the inclusion of technology within the classroom is done casually and does not essentially meet the needs of the 21st-century learner (Ertmer & Ottenbreit-Leftwich, 2010).

Within teacher professional development, teacher learning is vital and related to students' learning; there ought to be a link between teachers' proficiencies and understandings and students' learning (Welch, 2012). Hence, learning opportunities for teachers ought to be created to inspire technology-enabled pedagogy. Also, to teach within 21st-century classrooms, teachers ought to be aware of developing trends in education, technology-enabled pedagogy and responsive pedagogic tools. Moreover, teachers ought to possess the necessary skills to teach within 21st-century classrooms; they ought to be technology savvy (Boholano, 2017).

As was evident, there is a need to assist teachers in acquiring these necessary skills. To learn these skills, teachers are required to undergo professional development to use digital tools effectively as they embrace the Fourth Industrial Revolution. There are a variety of digital tools accessible globally (Buzzard, Crittenden, Crittenden, & McCarty, 2011), for the purpose of this study, digital tools refer to software and platforms for teaching and learning that may be used with computers or mobile devices. Additionally, the Internet[4] provides teachers with access to digital tools and social networking sites, and these sites offer the user the opportunity to invite other users to join these networks (Boholano, 2017).

Through the use of these networks, for example, Google classroom, Edmodo, TedEd and so on, students are provided with the chance to articulate their ideas, discuss their successes and challenges, work collaboratively, students also enhance their critical thinking skills and their skills of self-reflection and thereby construct meaningful knowledge (Jovanovic, Chiong, & Weise, 2012).

3   Theoretical Considerations: Exploring the Notions of Connectivism

Computers are essential in facilitating learning within the 21st-century classroom, and currently, institutions globally are introducing computer-supported learning and distance education courses to 21st-century students (Foroughi, 2015). Thus, within 21st-century education contexts, technology plays a substantial role in how we learn and how we conduct our everyday lives (Vululleh, 2018). New developments in technology-enabled pedagogy have provided more access for teachers to introduce a diverse array of technology-based tools and interactive technology-based learning approaches within the 21st-century classroom (Bailey, 2019).

However, to enhance the effectiveness of technology-enabled pedagogy, teachers ought to use technology effectively to support students' learning (Nami & Vaezi, 2018). The introduction of technology-enabled pedagogy into the learning environment, and the swift advances in technology, has led to the advancement of the theory of connectivism (Goldie, 2016). Connectivism is recommended as an applicable theory for learning within the digital age (Foroughi, 2015) since connectivism is a network learning theory which is guided by the notion that learning is a process whereby new information is continuously being acquired (Siemens, 2005).

Within the ambits of this framework, learners are allowed to use digital platforms, for example, social networking sites, blogs and online learning communities to discuss and develop knowledge (Goldie, 2016). The concept of networking is significant to connectivism since knowledge is perceived as moving from a network of humans to a network of machines (Bell, 2009). Hence, connectivism refers to networked social learning (Duke, Harper, & Johnson, 2013) and focuses on disseminated learning which is influenced by technology and the notion that learning may dwell within non-human applications (Goldie, 2016). Connectivism thus allows for a community of individuals working with technology-based tools to justify what they are undertaking (Bell, 2009).

4   Research Design and Methods

This qualitative study which sought to explore mathematics teachers' experiences on the use of technology-enabled pedagogy for transforming their classroom context was located within an interpretive paradigm. Data were generated via an interactive workshop and semi-structured interviews.

4.1   *Ethical Issues*
Gatekeeper access was acquired from the research office of the participating university. Participants were provided with an informed consent form detailing the purpose and process of the research study. To assure participants of their anonymity, names were not used, but rather the code 'P' and a number was assigned to represent each participant.

4.2   *The Participants*
The population for the study were postgraduate mathematics education students and lecturers. The postgraduate students were also mathematics school teachers. Thirty-eight participants were invited to participate in the study, and 29 responded positively. Five participants were randomly selected to

participate in the pilot study. Twenty four participants participated in the main study. Data were generated through an interactive workshop and semi-structured interview schedules.

4.3 *The Pilot Study*

Conducting the pilot study workshop and semi-structured interviews increased the validity and reliability of the research process. During the pilot study, some participants were uncertain of what was required of them for certain questions during the interview process. Subsequently, questions were rephrased to eliminate ambiguity and to ensure that each question was understandable. The language used during the workshop and interview process was focused and well-defined to improve the dependability and validity of the research instrument and research process.

4.4 *The Research Process and Tools*

4.4.1 The Workshop

One workshop focusing on technology-enabled pedagogy was conducted with the participants. The researcher facilitated the workshop and the participants were provided with teaching notes, presentations of case studies, lesson plans and assessments focusing on the effective integration of technology-enabled pedagogy within mathematics classrooms. Moreover, the workshop focused on using technology-enabled pedagogy with a view of embracing the Fourth Industrial Revolution.

PowerPoint Presentations, videos and the document camera[5] were used during these interactive workshops. At the end of the workshop, all participants were invited to one on one semi-structured interviews scheduled on dates a few months after the workshop. This meant that each participant would have the opportunity of reflecting on what they had learned from the workshop with the view of advancing their own pedagogy and thereby promoting their professional development. The interviews were designed to gauge the experiences of each participant on the use of technology-enabled pedagogy to transform their classroom context.

4.4.2 The Semi-Structured Interviews

Although 24 participants attended the workshop, due to work, study, personal or family commitments, only 15 participants were available to be interviewed. The interviews were audiotaped and transcribed verbatim. Transcripts were sent to participants for inspection to ensure the accuracy and validity of the interview transcripts. The purpose of the interview was to establish the participants' experiences of technology-enabled pedagogy with the view of transforming their classroom context to embrace the Fourth Industrial Revolution.

Each interview lasted between 30 to 45 minutes. The interviews were conducted at a venue and time that was suitable for each participant. Each interview began with a few general questions to place the participant at ease, the interview then progressed to specific questions focusing on the participant's experiences of the use of technology-enabled pedagogy for the 21st-century classroom. The findings of this study offer significant information for teacher professional development within the ambits of embracing the Fourth Industrial Revolution.

4.5 *Data Analysis*

Data analysis in the form of coding and categorizing of themes were based on the theoretical framework of the study, i.e. the theory of connectivism. Data analysis included the following steps: acquaintance with the data to classify codes after reading and rereading the qualitative data; refining the codes into themes; arranging segments of the data that were related to each other, and studying the data excerpts to warrant that the excerpts revealed a connection. Hence, three phases of coding were used to analyze the data generated.

Firstly, open coding was used to analyze the data. The purpose of this type of open coding was to reveal the experiences of participants focusing on the use of technology-enabled pedagogy within 21st-century classroom contexts. Secondly, all data was re-examined using a list of anticipated codes and themes focusing on each participant's responses regarding transforming their classroom context with the notion of embracing the Fourth Industrial Revolution. Finally, the similarities and difference between the participants' responses were compared. Also, member checking was done to confirm the accuracy of findings and to provide participants with the chance to correct and make additions to the data generated. A detailed discussion focusing on the findings of this study may be found in the section that follows.

5 Findings and Discussion

While in general, the participants valued the integration of technology within the classroom context, they did indicate that they had misgivings and experienced problems when attempting to replicate what they had learnt during the workshop. The participants' responses are captured in the discussions that follow.

5.1 Limitations of Using Technology-Enabled Pedagogy

5.1.1 The Lack of Material Resources Inhibits Technology-Enabled Pedagogy

Participants tried imitating demonstrations and experiences from the workshop; however, some of the participants had challenges due to the lack of infrastructure or resources at their schools to facilitate technology-enabled pedagogy within their classrooms. These notions are supported by excerpts from the interview transcripts that follow.

> P10 : …I could not access the suitable video that was linked to the lesson I was teaching…I copied the link at home…the Internet connection did not work at school…
>
> P15: …it seemed like a good idea…combining of technology and the chalkboard…the school does not have a working data projector…Internet access is limited…I used this for certain tasks…but using the Internet in class needs to be approved by the principal first…
>
> P23: …I reflected on what I was exposed to during the workshop. I realized that while it would be beneficial for my class, we do not have Internet access or the appropriate gadgets at school…I was not willing to use my phone it is too expensive to download presentations I can't use my data for Internet access…

Along similar lines, within the ambits of connectivism, learners ought to be supported by the teacher or a non-human appliance (Kizito, 2016). However, the lack of material resources may hinder teachers while they attempt to incorporate aspects of the 21st-century classroom within their milieus. The preceding transcript excerpts indicate that teachers are willing to embrace the Fourth Industrial Revolution. Teachers have a desire to integrate technology within their classroom milieus; however, the lack of material resources affects the teacher's ability and inspiration in introducing technology-enabled learning within their classrooms (Klopfer, Osterweil, Groff, & Haas, 2006).

The effective integration of technology within education forms an integral part of a 21st-century classroom (Boothe & Clarke, 2014; Cloete, 2017) and technology is vital for embracing the Fourth Industrial Revolution (4IR). Relevant role-players within educational milieus ought to collaborate to ensure that classrooms are adequately equipped with the necessary resources required to embrace the 4IR.

5.1.2 The Lack of Teacher Professional Development Inhibits Technology-Enabled Pedagogy

The effective integration of technology-enabled pedagogy is an essential aspect of teacher professional development; teachers need to know how to use technology for instruction (Ertmer & Ottenbreit-Leftwich, 2012). In this study, some participants indicated that they did not possess the know-how to integrate technology effectively during instruction. This notion is exemplified in the transcript excerpts that follow.

> P3: ...I just did not know how to link with my teaching...I had a mixture of technology and the board...I saw the demonstration at the workshop, but I could not do the same in my class...
> P13: ...I could only show the class the video, and I could explain how it was related to my maths topic...I could just do a visual activity and relate to their classwork or homework, but I did not know how to go further...
> P18: ...I use the technology to enter marks...submit to the department...I don't know how to search for maths links and videos...
> P19: ...need help to use technology tools...it is useful for learning...I need someone to show me how to develop teaching tasks using technology...

As was evident, teacher professional development activities focusing on using information communication technology (ICT) for teaching within differing classroom contexts is needed (Dlamini & Mbatha, 2018). So while connectivism may be used to transform learning activities (Kizito, 2016), teachers require professional development to become innovative and at ease with the integration and use of ICT as they teach their students within classroom contexts (Scott & Scott, 2010).

5.1.3 Technology-Enabled Pedagogy Causes Distractions in the Classroom

Although the participants welcomed the use of technology-enabled pedagogy, they also experienced challenges with the use of technology in their classrooms. They realized that the integration of technology within their classroom milieus created distractions in their classroom contexts. This notion is supported by the transcript excerpts that follow.

> P10: ...I was trying to access the video...I was not paying attention to the class...my learners were doing other activities and talking...a lot of lesson time was lost...I could not make my class pay attention to my lesson...
> P14: ...they became noisy and did not listen...they thought it was exciting...videos in class...very difficult to get their [the learners][6] attention...
> P24: ...I allowed them [the learners] to use cell phones in class...I arranged permission with the principal to use the school Internet...the class was very distracted...did not pay attention...went on Facebook[7] and WhatsApp[8]...difficult to get them to focus on the lesson...they were sending messages to each other in class...and were not listening to me...

Along similar lines, research (Goundar, 2014) supports the notion that the use of technology-based tools causes distractions and disruptions within the classroom context. Thus, teachers are required to carefully monitor and observe the interactions between students as they engage with digital tools. This implies that teachers need to ensure that they manage their classrooms effectively to facilitate the success of technology-enabled pedagogy. Hence, if necessary, teachers ought to attend professional development workshops focusing on how to manage the class effectively while integrating technology when teaching within differing classroom contexts (Dlamini & Mbatha, 2018).

5.2   Strengths of Using Technology-Enabled Pedagogy

5.2.1   Technology-Enabled Pedagogy Saves Time in the Classroom

Based on the demonstrations that the participants participated in during the workshop, they were encouraged to use technology-enabled pedagogy. These participants valued the use of technology-enabled pedagogy. This notion was evident in the transcript excerpts that follow.

> P5: ...the PowerPoint presentation saved time in class...I could easily go back to slides to respond to queries...
> P11: ...for teaching geometry...I used Sketchpad[9]...I used less time to sketch the diagrams...I could go back to the sketch to assist my class with questions...it is more accurate to draw using this technology teaching tool...learners can visualize the transformations and manipulations...
> P16: ...I used transparencies and the overhead projector...I prepared the transparencies in advance...I could refer to the complex solutions for Geometry that the class needed...the diagrams became faster and easier to represent...
> P18: ...the videos supported me while I was teaching...the class could see the dimensions I was talking about...the visuals saved time...I had more time to give feedback to my class...

As was evident, technology-enabled pedagogy allowed the participants to teach their content in innovative and exciting ways. These participants were agents of change (Ertmer & Ottenbreit-Leftwich, 2010); they were transforming their classroom contexts to embrace the 4IR. These participants inspired their learners by exhibiting innovative strategies for students to visualize the mathematics being taught. Being able to visualize the mathematical concepts being taught inspires active learning (Shallcross & Harrison, 2007).

Moreover, within the ambits of connectivism, the learning environment is student-centered and focusses on engaging students in meaningful learning tasks (Kizito, 2016). Thus, technology-enabled pedagogy deepens students' understanding of concepts being taught and also enhances meaningful learning (Huang & Li, 2009).

5.2.2 Technology-Enabled Pedagogy Makes Abstract Mathematical Concepts Easier to Comprehend

The participants valued the use of technology-enabled pedagogy since this supported learners' understanding. The mathematics concepts being taught were easier to explain and were more manageable for the learners to grasp. Learners could continuously refer to the visuals and the videos being used in the class to support their meaning-making process. These views are supported by the transcript excerpts that follow.

> P6: …technology helped me to explain the maths concepts…when they [the learners] had a problem we could go back…it was efficient with technology…going back enabled me to reinforce what I was teaching… concepts became easier to understand…
>
> P8: …from the diagrams that we used with sketchpad learners understood the maths better…it was becoming easier…they [the learners] could see the maths being taught…
>
> P13: …as the class watched the video…they were enlightened…they now understood the mathematics concepts being taught…the learners answered the questions with ease…the video made the concepts easier for them [the learners] to understand…
>
> P24: …they [the learners] used their cell phones to probe the maths being taught…they were distracted…went on Facebook and WhatsApp…but at the end of the lesson they could answer questions and define what was being taught…technology made the maths being taught easier for them [the learners] to grasp…

Research (Murphy, 2016; Silin & Kwok, 2017) supports the notion that technology-enabled pedagogy is useful within the classroom environment as was evident, based on the findings of this study, the accessibly to technology allowed the participants to be innovative within their pedagogy (Bell, 2009). Moreover, within the ambits of connectivism, the use of technology-enabled pedagogy may be used to transform activities for learners (Kizito, 2016). This transformation of pedagogy made the abstract mathematics concepts (for example concepts revolving around proofs in Euclidean Geometry) being taught easier to understand.

5.2.3 Technology-Enabled Pedagogy Encourages Interaction and Collaboration

The participants used a blending teaching and learning approach, which incorporated the use of technology and the traditional 'chalk and talk' method. Based on the findings of this study, this type of approach encouraged interaction and collaboration within the classroom environment. This is supported by the transcript excerpt that follows.

> P7: ...I used the PowerPoint in the class...learners started discussing concepts with each other...more interactive...discussions were focused on the maths being taught...seemed to enjoy working with each other...
> P14: ...used WhatsApp to start discussions while they were away from class... in the classroom, the discussions continued...they enjoyed this type of teaching...it became more fruitful and interesting...learners took control...
> P15: ...experienced challenges...I had to get permission to use the Internet...I used a combination of the chalkboard and my computer...my learners became more talkative...worked together on problems...they seemed to learn better when working with each other...

As was evident, through the use of the blended teaching and learning approach, the participants made the learners responsible for their learning. Moreover, connecting learners and resources online does not necessarily take place in the classroom; this is ubiquitous due to our access to the Internet (Bell, 2009). This notion was supported by the participants' use of WhatsApp before the lesson commenced.

Through the blended teaching and learning approach, the learners collaborated and discussed solutions while the teacher facilitated. Collaboration is supported within the ambits of connectivism, student learning is enhanced by sharing and collaboration (Duke, Harper, & Johnson, 2013) and there is also room for individual learning (Kizito, 2016). Thus, this type of learning milieu is supported by the notions of connectivism, since connectivism promotes technology-enabled pedagogy whereby control for learning within the classroom shifts from the teacher to the learner (Foroughi, 2015).

6 Conclusion

This study aimed to explore mathematics teachers' experiences of using technology-enabled pedagogy for the 21st-century classroom. This qualitative, interpretive study was conducted at one university in KwaZulu-Natal, South

Africa. Participants were invited to an interactive workshop and were consequently interviewed. Two main themes surfaced from this study, Limitations of using technology-enabled pedagogy and strengths of using technology-enabled pedagogy. After the third stage of data coding, subthemes emerged: The lack of material resources inhibits technology-enabled pedagogy, the lack of teacher professional development inhibits technology-enabled pedagogy, and technology-enabled pedagogy causes distractions in the classroom. Technology-enabled pedagogy saves time in the classroom, makes abstract mathematical concepts easier to comprehend, and technology-enabled pedagogy encourages interaction and collaboration.

This study has provided some interesting experiences regarding the use of technology-enabled pedagogy to embrace the Fourth Industrial Revolution. It was evident that within contemporary classrooms, technology has the potential to improve pedagogy by providing individualized, real-time interactions among students and their teachers (Vululleh, 2018). This implies that teachers may employ the use of technology and social networks within their pedagogy to enhance meaningful learning within and outside the 21st-century classroom.

Moreover, based on the findings of this study it is apparent that within the 21st-century classroom as technology becomes more available and if connectivism is embraced as a useful framework within the Fourth Industrial Revolution, teachers will seek to engage in supportive pedagogy to amplify the benefits to student learning. This was evident since the participants within this study were willing to transform their traditional pedagogy to create collaborative and engaging technology-enriched classroom milieus to support their students' learning needs. However, for the successful integration of technology-enabled pedagogy within the 21st-century classroom, there is a need for teachers to be involved in professional development workshops focusing on how to enhance student learning while integrating technology within their pedagogy. These professional development workshops would of benefit to teachers globally as we embrace the Fourth Industrial Revolution.

Acknowledgement

This research was partially funded by the National Research Foundation: NRF Grant Number: UID 113952.

Notes

1   The words teacher and lecturer are used synonymously in this chapter.
2   The words learner and student are used synonymously in this chapter.

3   The words classroom and lecture room are used synonymously in this chapter.
4   The Internet is a global system of interconnected computer networks that consists of private, public, academic, business, and government networks linked by electronic, wireless, and optical networking technologies.
5   A document camera is a contemporary replacement for the overhead transparency projector and allows the user to project documents or objects digitally.
6   Words in square brackets within the transcripts have been added by the researcher to support the reader's understanding.
7   Facebook is a social networking site that provides one with the opportunity to connect and share information online with friends, colleagues and family.
8   WhatsApp is a free app that you may download on your cell phone, iPad or computer. WhatsApp uses the Internet to send or share messages, images or video.
9   Sketchpad is a type of dynamic geometry software that may be used to teach geometry in the classroom.

References

Bailey, L. W. (2019). New technology for the classroom: Mobile devices, Artificial Intelligence, tutoring systems, and robotics. In *Educational technology and the new world of persistent learning*. University of Phoenix.

Bell, F. (2009). Connectivism: A network theory for teaching and learning in a connected world. *University of Salford, 1*(1), 1–7.

Boholano, H. B. (2017). Smart social networking: 21st century teaching and learning skills. *Research in Pedagogy, 7*(1), 21–29. doi:10.17810/2015.45

Boothe, D., & Clark, L. (2014). *The 21st century classroom: Creating a culture of innovation in ICT*. https://conference.pixel-online.net/ICT4LL/files/ict4ll/ed0007/FP/0475-ICL733-FP-ICT4LL7.pdf

Borko, H. (2004). Professional development and teacher learning: Mapping the terrain. *Educational Researcher, 33*(8), 3–15.

Buzzard, C., Crittenden, V. L., Crittenden, W. F., & McCarty, P. (2011). The use of digital technologies in the classroom: A teaching and learning perspective. *Journal of Marketing Education, 33*(2), 131–139. doi:10.1177/0273475311410845

Clemmons, R. (2013, May). *Technology, instruction and the 21st century classroom.* http://www.edtechmagazine.com/higher/article/2013/05/technology-ins

Cloete, A. L. (2017). Technology and education: Challenges and opportunities. *HTS Teologiese Studies/Theological Studies, 73*(4), 1–7. doi:10.4102/hts.v73i4.4589

Darling-Hammond, L. (2017). Teacher education around the world: What can we learn from international practice? *European Journal of Teacher Education, 40*(3), 291–309. doi:10.1080/02619768.2017.1315399

Duke, B., Harper, G., & Johnson, M. (2013). *Connectivism as a digital age learning theory.* https://www.hetl.org/wp-content/uploads/2013/09/HETLReview2013SpecialIssueArticle1.pdf

Ertmer, A. P., & Ottenbreit-Leftwich, T. A. (2010). Teacher technology change: How knowledge, confidence, beliefs, and culture intersect. *Journal of Research on Technology in Education, 42*(3), 255–284. doi:10.1080/15391523.2010.10782551

Ertmer, A. P., & Ottenbreit-Leftwich, A. (2012). Removing obstacles to the pedagogical changes required by Jonassen's vision of authentic technology-enabled learning. *Computers & Education, 64*(1), 175–182. doi:10.1016/j.compedu.2012.10.008

Foroughi, A. (2015). The theory of connectivism: Can it explain and guide learning in the digital age? *Journal of Higher Education and Practice, 15*(5), 11–26.

Goertz, P. (2015). *10 signs of a 21st century classroom*. George Lucas Educational Foundation.

Goldie, J. G. S. (2016). Connectivism: A knowledge learning theory for the digital age. *Medical Teacher, 38*(10), 1064–1069. doi:10.3109/0142159X.2016.1173661

Goundar, S. (2014). The distraction of technology in the classroom. *Journal of Education & Human Development, 3*(1), 211–229. http://jehdnet.com/journals/jehd/Vol_3_No_1_March_2014/14.pdf

Huang, R., & Li, Y. (2009). Examining the nature of effective teaching through master teachers' lesson evaluation in China. In J. Cai, G. Kaiser, B. Perry, & N.-Y. Wong (Eds.), *Effective mathematics teaching from teachers' perspectives. National and crossnational studies* (pp. 163–181). Sense Publishers.

Jovanovic, J., Chiong, R., & Weise, T. (2012). Social networking, teaching and learning. *Interdisciplinary Journal of Information, Knowledge, and Management, 7*(1), 39–43. http://ftp.jrc.es/EURdoc/JRC55629.pdf

Kizito, R. N. (2016). Connectivism in learning activity design: Implications for pedagogically-based technology adoption in African Higher Education contexts. *International Review of Research in Open and Distributed Learning, 17*(2), 19–39. https://doi.org/10.19173/irrodl.v17i2.2217

Klopfer, E., Osterweil, S., Groff, J., & Haas, J. (2006). Using the technology of today, in the classroom today. The instructional power of digital games, social networking simulations and how teachers can leverage them. In *The educational arcade*. Creative Commons, Massachusetts Institute of Technology.

Lalima, D., & Dangwal, K. L. (2017). Blended learning: An innovative approach. *Universal Journal of Educational Research, 5*(1), 129–136. https://files.eric.ed.gov/fulltext/EJ1124666.pdf

Murphy, D. (2016). A literature review: The effect of implementing technology in a high school mathematics classroom. *International Journal of Research in Education and Science (IJRES), 2*(2), 295–299.

Nami, F., & Vaezi, S. (2018). How ready are our students for technology-enhanced learning? Students at a university of technology respond. *Journal of Computing in Higher Education, 30*(1), 510–529. doi:10.1007/s12528-018-9181-5

Schwab, K. (2016). *The Fourth Industrial Revolution*. World Economic Forum.

Scott, D. E., & Scott, S. (2010). Innovations in the use of technology and teacher professional development. In J. O. Lindberg & A. D. Olofsson (Eds.), *Online learning communities and teacher professional development: Methods for improved education delivery* (pp. 169–189). IGI Global.

Shallcross, D. E., & Harrison, T. G. (2007). Lectures: electronic presentations versus chalk and talk – A chemist's view. *Chemistry Education Research and Practice, 8*(1), 73–79. https://www.rsc.org/images/Shallcross%20paper%20final_tcm18-76282.pdf

Siemens, G. (2005). Connectivism: A learning theory for the digital age. *International Journal of Technology and Distance Learning, 1*(1), 1–9. http://www.itdl.org/Journal/Jan_05/article01.htm

Silin, Y., & Kwok, D. (2017). A study of students' attitudes towards using ICT in a social constructivist environment. *Australasian Journal of Educational Technology, 33*(5), 50–62. https://doi.org/10.14742/ajet.2890

Vululleh, P. (2018). Determinants of students' e-learning acceptance in developing countries: An approach based on Structural Equation Modeling (SEM). *International Journal of Education and Development using ICT, 14*(1), 141–151. https://www.learntechlib.org/p/183560/

Welch, T. (2012). *Teacher development: What works and how can we learn from this and maximize the benefits?* Presentation at the Teachers' Upfront meeting. Wits School of Education, South Africa.

PART 3

The 21st-Century Teacher

CHAPTER 6

Teaching and Assessment Skills Needed by 21st-Century Teachers: Embracing the Fourth Industrial Revolution

Septimi Kitta and Jaquiline Amani

Abstract

Today, as never before, the world is experiencing rapid transformation accompanied by knowledge-driven economies, information exchange and technological advancement and innovations, which has created a global shift in educational goals in pedagogy, the curriculum and assessment. By using secondary sources, this chapter highlights the key competencies and skills that teachers need in the 21st century for them to teach and assess effectively. The authors draw on the experiential learning theory by Kolb, the constructivist approach to learning and Singapore's 21st-century Model for teaching professionals to answer the basic question: *"What makes the 21st-century teacher different from previous centuries in terms of instructional and assessment skills?"* Specifically, we examined what 21st-century teachers need to know (knowledge) and do (skills) to prepare students to respond to the demands of the Fourth Industrial Revolution. Our critical review of the literature is based on seven sub-themes namely: Student-centered teaching, differentiated instruction, linking technology, content and pedagogy, the role of professional ethics and values, assessing skills beyond knowledge, performance-based assessment and the adoption of multiple assessment tools for varied skills. Based on our review, we conclude that 21st-century teachers need to be lifelong learners to enable their students to meet the labor market demands in the era of the Fourth Industrial Revolution. Indeed, as Information and Communications Technology has become an important tool in the 21st-century, teachers need to apply innovative teaching and assessment approaches that personalize learning, while providing students with hands-on skills. Lastly, we emphasize that character-building needs to be an integral part of education provision at all levels to prepare our students for global citizenship.

1   Introduction

Education is crucial for any society, and its effectiveness is reflected in its strengths and weaknesses, both domestically and abroad. It involves the experience that a person acquires inside and outside the classroom. Türkkahraman (2012) argue that for a society to be successful in competing economically in the world, education is fundamental and is impacted by economics, advances in scientific technology and industrial knowledge, amongst others. The major aims of education are to prepare and equip learners with relevant skills and competences so that they contribute substantially to the well-being of society. This training provides individuals with the requisite skills, good morals and tolerance, which promotes co-existence and the nation's development (Okogbaa, 2017).

Today, as never before, the world is experiencing rapid transformation accompanied by technological advancement and innovations, which has raised questions as to what skills our young people and teachers need in response to this, and what and how students should learn to function effectively in the era of the Fourth Industrial Revolution. The reason for these questions is that employers are concerned about whether the competencies of school leavers or graduates will be of use to them and contribute to society (Care, Kim, Vista, & Anderson, 2018; Price, Pierson, & Light, 2011).

A thorough analysis of research by Chalkiadaki (2018), Voogt and Roblin (2012) and Care (2018) revealed that the core frameworks for skills needed by 21st-century learners are: Partnership for 21st-century skills; Assessment and Teaching of 21st-Century Skills (ATCS) (Binkley et al., 2012); EnGauge 21st-century skills (Lemke et al., 2003); 21st-Century Skills and Competencies for the new millennium learners (Organization for Economic Co-operation and Development [OECD], 2005); Key competences for lifelong learning, Information and Communications Technology (ICT) competency framework for teachers (United Nations Educational, Scientific and Cultural Organization [UNESCO], 2008a). In addition, Care and Kim (2018) reported on large-scale mapping research by UNESCO supported by NEQMAP in 102 countries. The findings revealed the attempts made to identify specific skills for the 21st-century in vision and mission statements, curricula, policies and educational plans. For example, 86% of the sampled countries agreed on the need to have young people who are problem solvers, good communicators, evidence-based decision-makers, and creative thinkers. A report by UNESCO (2015) on nine countries in the Asia-Pacific region documented the competencies they needed at policy and practice levels, whereby four were found to dominate, namely communication, creativity, critical thinking and problem-solving, as well as interpersonal skills, intrapersonal skills, global citizenship and computer literacy. A good number of these skills are in the cognitive and social domains (Care, 2018). Basically, these studies agree on the need for the rationale of teaching and learning beyond traditional pedagogical practices (Care, 2018; Price, Pierson, & Light, 2011; Care & Kim, 2018).

In view of these global changes, Tanzania reviewed its curricula for basic education, that is, primary education and ordinary level secondary education. This took place between 2004 and 2008. Apart from basic education, advanced secondary education and teacher education curricula were also reviewed. This was necessitated by the need for the education systems to prepare school leavers who are ready in solving socio-economic challenges in terms knowledge, skills and attitudes (Ministry of Education and Vocational Training [MoEVT], 2010). This is because of the realization that the "education system could no longer ignore the skills necessary for employment and academic and social survival in the modern world" (Paulo & Tilya, 2014, p. 114). According to Mkimbili and Kitta (2020), the reviewed curriculum was aimed at enabling pupils to acquire competencies for meeting the demands of the 21st century, and ensuring that teachers use interactive, participatory teaching and learning approaches in a child-friendly environment. "In the curriculum, seven 21st-century skills were emphasized, namely, communication, numeracy, creativity, critical thinking, technology, interpersonal relationships and independent learning" (Mkimbili & Kitta, 2019, p. 64).

However, the biggest challenge is teachers' ability to design classroom learning that imparts 21st-learning skills. The authors used Kolb's (1984), constructivist approach to learning theory, and Singapore's 21st-Model for the teaching profession to assess whether or not teachers have the necessary skills to teach effectively in the 21st century. Specifically, we addressed the question, *"What makes the 21st-century teacher different from previous centuries in terms of instructional and assessment skills?"* We adopted the teacher education model for the 21st century from the Singapore National Institute of Education (NIE) to gain insights into how well teachers are prepared. The Teacher Education Model for 21st century (TE21 Model) was developed in 2009 to guide the design, delivery and evaluation of education programs, whereby learners are at the *heart* of education goals (NIE, 2009).

This means that the teaching process should consider the diverse needs of the students. The TE21 Model underscores the essential knowledge and skills that should be possessed by our teachers in light of the contemporary global dynamics in order to improve student outcomes. In an attempt to provide a theoretical foundation on how to produce a "thinking teacher", TE21 Model considers the underpinning philosophy, curriculum, desired outcomes for our teachers, and academic pathways as key elements of teacher education (Schleicher, 2012). Moreover, the competences for the 21st century aspiring teaching professionals are viewed in a holistic manner whose development process results from a combination of various pillars such as, the pedagogies, assessment, values, skills and knowledge (NIE, 2009). These interrelated elements are considered the potential for addressing the 21st-century classroom challenges. Indeed, a balance between theory-practice nexus is of paramount importance whereby the TE21 Model proposes the adoption of experiential learning, reflection, and school-based inquiry or research as the suitable approaches to provide students with hands-on skills before they join the world of work.

2 Methodology

Drawing on secondary sources to draw inferences from existing data on the subject being researched (Steward & Kamins, 1993), this chapter analyzes the skills needed by a 21st-century teacher to effectively teach and assess 21st-century learners. Taking into consideration the aim of the study, the peer-reviewed journal articles, electronic and printed books, unpublished Master Dissertations and international reports on 21st-century skills were searched. Secondary research data is usually analyzed to obtain information which may influence the conclusions drawn (Steward & Kamins, 1993; Bryman, 2012). We chose to analyze what was relevant in the collected data, based on the research question, which was then interpreted and analyzed through content analysis. Accordingly, the authors reviewed 27 Journal articles, 12 book chapter, two unpublished Master Dissertations, one (1) national report and three international reports. The analysis further revealed that only 17 Journal articles and eight book chapters offered close themes which were related to the research questions.

Key themes which were found to be relevant for discussion include pedagogical practices, assessment skills, values and ethical dimensions. These themes were then expanded as factors explaining the main research questions with support from empirical evidence from previous research. These were (i) 21st-century teaching strategies and approaches, (ii) Strategies for assessing 21st-century skills. (iii) The role of teachers' professional ethics in teaching and assessing 21st-century skills (see Figure 6.1). Under pedagogical strategies, we characterized effective 21st-century teacher is one who places the learners at the core of the learning process, considers their diversity and needs while linking the technology with the content and pedagogy. Furthermore, our conceptualization of the 21st-century teacher under assessment package was centered on three key assessment practices. These include; use assessment as a tool to

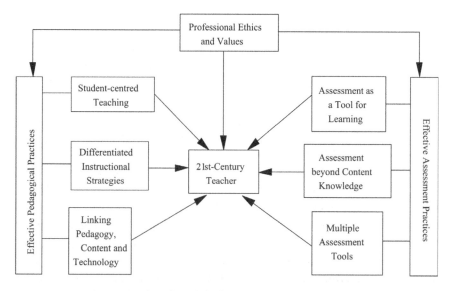

FIGURE 6.1   21st-century teachers' knowledge base: A conceptual framework (based on Anangisye, 2010; Binkley et al., 2012; Care, 2018; Chowdhury, 2016; Daisy, 2015; Kolb, 2014; NIE, 2009; Schleicher, 2012; Rasheed & Wahid, 2018; The American Association of Colleges for Teacher Education [AACTE], 2008; UNESCO, 2008a)

enhance learning, assessment beyond the content knowledge, and role of multiple assessment tools. Professional ethics was conceived as the intermediate frame, in which, its presence is critical for the quality realization of effective pedagogical and assessment practices. We analyze and discuss how each of these factors accounts for the knowledge-base and skills of the 21st-century teachers in the next section.

3   Findings and Discussion

3.1   *Strategies for Imparting Skills for the 21st Century*

The introduction to this chapter provides an understanding of what skills our children need to acquire to enable them to cope with the demands and challenges of the 21st century, based on frameworks established worldwide. It also shows that the challenges facing most surveyed countries are teachers knowing how best to translate the vision, mission statement and curriculum into what students are capable of learning and how they should learn it, what teachers need to teach and how to assess students (Care, 2018), which calls for teachers' approaches to learning to be scrutinised. The following section analyses the student-centered approach to teaching.

3.1.1 Student-Centered Teaching

There has been a global shift in educational provision, from traditional instructional practices to innovative ways of teaching, which put the student as a focus of teaching and learning process. Care and Kim (2018) argue, therefore, that this interactive style of pedagogy needs teachers with 21st-century skills. Moreover, Blomeke et al. (2015) assert that teachers need these skills to enable students to acquire competencies applicable to their lives, which means that our teachers need to use relevant learning approaches to fulfil this important goal.

One approach that has contributed to our understanding of how students learn is constructivism (Olusegun, 2015). Drawing on the work of Piaget (1890), Dewey (1929) and Vygotsky (1962), the constructivists view the learner as an active participant in the acquisition of knowledge. This means that for learning to be meaningful, students should participate in the construction of knowledge so that what they learn has come from their experience, i.e. student-centered learning (Olusegun, 2015). As they do this, they will create their own image of the real world and will update their mental model to take in and interpret the new information received (Driscoll, 2000).

Constructivism is similar to Kolb's experiential learning theory. In his book titled experiential learning as a source of learning and development, he argues that consciousness and experience play a central role in the learning process, whereby gaining knowledge is a continuous process tested out in the experience of the learner. So it is a process and not an outcome (Kolb, 2014). Through this approach, students have the opportunity to actively participate in learning through reflecting on it, in order to apply what they have learnt to different situations, in and outside the classroom.

Both these approaches to learning agree that learning is a process that is linked to what students already know. Thus in the classroom, teachers can create a learning environment which allows students to resolve their real-life problems by conducting research, sharing their findings, receiving feedback and reflecting on what has or has not worked. Teachers may give students activities based on the subject to enable them to create new knowledge based on their previous understanding. To achieve this, problem-based learning, laboratory experiments, case-based learning, cooperative learning and inquiry-based learning can be used. In groups, for example, students will have the opportunity to explore what they already know, their current learning needs, and sources of knowledge to solve existing problems.

3.1.2 Differentiated Instruction

Contemporary classrooms are increasingly being populated by students who are diverse (Lawrence-Brown, 2004; Subban, 2006), which means that educators are compelled to adopt instructional strategies that respond to a different learners' needs, known as *"differentiated instruction"*. According to Tomlinson (2005), this is a philosophy of teaching which view effective learning as a function of teachers' ability to accommodate students' differences in terms of their readiness to learn, language and interests. With differentiated instruction, the structure, management and content of the classroom will benefit all students (Subban, 2006). Learners need differentiated instruction because they do not learn in the same manner (Subban, 2006; Rasheed & Wahid, 2018).

While educators agree that learners' needs are diverse, a good number of teachers do not accommodate these differences in teaching and learning process (Gable, Hendrickson, Tonelson, & Van Acker, 2000), which might affect students' readiness to learn, thereby lowering their academic performance. Therefore, teachers are encouraged to apply the best strategies for their context so as to develop the skills needed for the 21st century. Diana (2004), Subban (2006), Vaughn, Bos, and Schumm (2000) propose several ways in which teachers can effectively adopt differentiated instruction. Getting additional support to enable struggling students to achieve learning goals as per the curriculum, such as the assistance of other students or teachers, is one way. Others are to emphasize the most important skills, to make a connection with prior knowledge/experience, to use an enriched curriculum for gifted students, and to fully engage students to make sure that the curriculum is positively connected to their lives.

3.1.3 Linking Technology, Content and Pedagogy

The 21st century has witnessed a global transformation in Information and Communications Technology (ICT), which impacts how we use it, especially as education systems are not immune to this technological transformation. Since the global economies strive to maintain productivity and embrace technological advances, equipping students with ICT skills is necessary for them to fully participate and succeed in today's information-rich, technology-driven society (Kozma, 2011). Today, with technological advances, learners can access the content learnt or to be learnt on various search engines inside and outside the classroom. According to the Assessment and Teaching of 21st-Century Skills project done in 60 institutions worldwide, ICT is categorized as a working tool for the 21st-century labor market (Binkley et al., 2010). Thus, teachers need to be agents of innovation because technology keeps on changing. They need to acquire and use technological skills not only to teach but also to manage and track students' learning outcomes. To help them do so, two guidelines were developed in 2008 to integrate ICT in education, namely Technological Pedagogical Content Knowledge (TPACK) (Thompson & Mishra, 2007) and ICT competency framework (UNESCO, 2008a).

The TPACK guides the kind of knowledge needed by teachers to integrate technology in the content, and to help them understand the relationship between technology, pedagogy and content (The American Association of Colleges for Teacher Education [AACTE], 2008; Mishra, & Koehler, 2006). It builds on Shulman's construct of Pedagogical Content Knowledge (PCK) to include technology knowledge as situated within the content and pedagogical knowledge (Mishra & Koehler, 2006; Schmidt-Crawford et al., 2009). Thus, 21st-century teachers need to know how to align new technologies with content and pedagogy and creatively use them to meet students' diverse learning needs (AACTE, 2008). UNESCO (2008a) also developed an ICT competency framework to identify the qualifications teachers need to integrate ICT in teaching and learning. For ICT to be integrated to achieve the best quality pedagogy and mastery of 21st-century skills, macro and micro initiatives are needed. At the macro level, the government needs to invest in the infrastructure needed and in building the capacity of teachers. In contrast, at the micro-level teachers need to be able to apply the technology to how they teach and assess students.

3.1.4 The Role of Professional Ethics and Values

It has become apparent that fast-moving ICT has compelled education systems throughout the world to access knowledge through it, which is the main thrust of the 21st-century. Research has shown that with the rapid technological transformation, it is imperative to nurture our students morally, intellectually, physically and socially (Chowdhury, 2016; Hameed, 2011). To inculcate morals, values and ethics in students, we also need teachers with the same characteristics, who are aware of and abide by their professional ethics. Sherpa (2018) explains that "teaching is a noble profession as it creates good quality human resources, responsible citizens, socialized and creative individuals" (p. 16). Therefore, teachers need to be committed to their institution and learners (Sherpa, 2018). Campbell (2003) cited in Anangisye (2010) maintains that a teacher should be a moral person and educator, who is to guide students to live a moral life. This is vitally important because, as Schaeffer (1999) says, "when teachers provide character education, they will be inculcating in students important ethical values, such as caring, honesty, fairness, a sense of responsibility and respect for self and others" (p. 3).

Daisy (2015) put forward four ethical values that are linked to the standard of teaching, knowledge, skills, competence and conduct, which are: (a) Respect, which presupposes that teachers should uphold human dignity and promote equality and emotional and cognitive development. In their professional practice, teachers should demonstrate respect for spiritual and cultural values, diversity, social justice, freedom, democracy and the environment; (b) Integrity, which entails honesty, reliability and moral action, demonstrated through the commitment, sense of responsibility and actions of teachers; (c) Care, whereby teachers bear in mind the best interests of the learners entrusted to their care, by showing empathy and making professional judgments; and (d) Trust, on which teachers' relationship with pupils, colleagues, parents, the school management and the public are based. It also embodies fairness, openness and honesty (p. 73).

In Tanzania, various scholars have widely researched on teachers' ethics. Their findings revealed the prevalence of teachers' misconduct in various schools and the proposed mitigation strategies (Anangisye, 2011), teachers and educators' practices which foster teacher ethics (Fussy, 2012) and teachers' awareness of their role as moral educators (Mdem, 2013). These studies underscore the importance of teachers' ethics and moral education for the delivery of quality education in Tanzania. Since teacher training institutions are entrusted with preparing good quality teachers, their programs should inculcate ethics and values in trainee students before they enter the teaching profession as graduates. Sirotnik (1990) argued that teacher education is more about building moral character than imparting knowledge-based skills and expertise. Although research praises the initiatives taken by teacher training institutions to use college regulations and religious codes of conduct, there is no course on teachers' ethics (Anangisye, 2010), which calls for the teacher education curriculum to be reviewed.

To conclude, having well-trained teachers with pedagogical skills and knowledge needed for the 21st century, who are either unethical or fail to impart moral and ethical values to pupils is like having a beautiful house with no foundations. Thus, teachers' ethical behavior is extremely important for successful teaching and learning. Teacher training institutions should focus on fundamental ethics, knowledge of the subject matter, innovation, teaching and assessment methods and imparting the skills needed in the 21st century.

3.2   *Strategies for Assessing the Skills Needed for the 21st Century*

It is maintained that for the education system to prepare students with the skills they need for both work and life in the 21st century, effective mechanisms are needed to assess them. The following sections present the strategies for enabling teachers to assess both cognitive and social skills effectively while tracking students' learning outcomes and progress. The strategies are (1) Assessment for Learning as the centrality of Learning (2) Assessment beyond Knowledge (3) Performance-based Assessment (4) Multiple Assessment tools which Measure Various Skills.

3.2.1 Assessment for Learning as the Centrality of 21st-Century Learning

The major goal of formative assessment is to improve students' learning outcomes and competence (Care & Kim, 2018; Anderson &, Palm 2017). It provides specific information about their strengths and difficulties, which will enable teachers to make informed decisions about what and how they teach (Peregrino, 2014; Black & William, 2009). On the other hand, the purpose of summative assessment is to determine whether or not educational standards have been met (Gotch & French, 2014), as well as gaps in students' learning and how far they have progressed (Isaacs, Zara, Herbert, Coombs, & Smith,2013). Whether the summative or formative assessment is used, the results should align with the intended learning goal (Vlachou, 2018).

Basically, the 21st-century skills require assessment practices which not only reveal how and what students know through paper-pencil medium but also assist the application of acquired competences in their work and life. In order to achieve this, assessment practices should be geared towards guiding teachers' actions and enabling students to gauge their learning progress (Perregrino, 2014). Therefore, assessment for learning seems to be a relevant practice as it supports ongoing teaching and learning. Students will also benefit from assessment, as it will show them where they have done well and where improvement is needed (Peregrino, 2014). As such, this would enable the contemporary students to evaluate the validity and relevance of what and how they learn from their own perspectives. They will gather information, make hypotheses and collect evidence to test them and come up with innovative ideas which will help them make sense of the world and function properly in their societies.

3.2.2 Assessment of Skills beyond Knowledge

Sustainable Development Goal four recognizes learning objectives across three categories, namely; cognitive socio-emotional and behavioral (UNESCO, 2015a). This implies that 21st-century teachers should go beyond assessing core knowledge and concepts to equipping students to apply them, thereby showing a clear association between what has been taught with the assessment (Care, 2018). It is asserted that assessment by teachers that is of a high quality enables them to assess students' skills and abilities beyond the content (Price, Pierson, & Light, 2011).

According to Gulikers et al. (2004), this assessment enables students to acquire information about their knowledge and skills to solve problems, have good communication skills, make evidence-based decisions, think creatively and apply what they have learnt to their socio-cultural contexts (Care et al., 2018). Gulikers et al. (2004) also insist that the results of the assessment must also reflect students' progress in learning, which means tracking the development of skills in different disciplines at various stages. Therefore, it is vital for teachers to have the skills needed to assess students across all these domains.

3.2.3 Performance-Based Assessment

One strategy for assessing higher-order skills is performance-based assessment (PBA) (Palm, 2008; Richards & Schmidt, 2002; VanTassel-Baska, 2013). PBA is aimed at finding out whether students have learnt what they should have by giving them a task to perform (Richards & Schmidt, 2002). In any subject matter in which performance-based assessment is used, it is basically an attempt to discover not only what students know about a topic and if they have capabilities to apply that knowledge in a "real-world" situation (Price, Pierson, & Light, 2011). Therefore, it is an alternative way of assessing students' ability (VanTassel-Baska, 2013), which does not depend on tests and examinations to measure their performance (Price, Pierson, & Light, 2011). Besides, it enables students to apply their knowledge and skills to different contexts that are likely to occur outside the classroom (Palm, 2008).

An example of performance-based assessment activities is designing and constructing a model based on any subject, conducting research and writing a report, doing a scientific experiment, and creating and testing a computer program (Darling-Hammond & Pecheone, 2009), which are tasks that simulate real-world challenges (Price, Pierson, & Light, 2011). PBA has many advantages over standard multiple-choice examinations. It enables teachers to make meaningful adjustments to their teaching (Darling-Hammond & Pecheone, 2009). Another benefit of PBA is that it is student-centered. Apart from being student-centered, PBA is very good at assessing higher-order thinking and other 21st-century skills (Price, Pierson, & Light, 2011), as well as allowing students to demonstrate their understanding (Darling-Hammond & Pecheone, 2009). More importantly, with PBA, it is easier to predict the future performance of learners (Yousefpoori-Naeim, 2014). However, the authors' emphasis on performance-based tasks does not mean replacing standardized tests. The adoption of performance-based assessment should be informed by the purpose of testing and nature of the skill to be measured. As VanTassel-Baska (2013) insist if the examiners assess the mastery of the content in a given subject matter, paper-and-pencil test with close-ended items may be preferable unlike higher-order thinking and problem solving which performance-based approach sounds more appropriate.

For performance-based assessment to be authentic, the following aspects need to be taken into consideration (Gulikers et al., 2004):

– Activities which relates to professional practice;
– The physical context reflects the mechanism in which the competencies will be applied in professional practice;
– The reflection of the application of social processes (if relevant) in the real situation; and,
– Criteria to identify and indicate the expected level of performance.

However, Care and Kim (2018) caution that for an assessment to be authentic, it must measure what it purports to measure and have supporting evidence. Therefore, in line with Gulikers et al. (2004), teachers should produce evidence of learning from the tasks students are given that reflect their competences.

3.2.4 Multiple Assessment Tools Which Measure Various Skills

It has been empirically established that no single assessment, whether formative or summative, can evaluate all learning outcomes (Pellegrino, 2014). As such, it is worth envisioning multiple assessment tools for different assessment purposes. According to Pellegrino (2014), the use of multiple assessment tools will bring complementary data for reasoned decisions about what and how the students learn. Price, Pierson and Light (2011) proposed tools for assessing learning and the skills acquired, such as rubrics, portfolios, performance-based assessments and self-and peer-assessment. However, Chu, Reynods, Tavares, Notari, and Lee (2017) warn that the wider the range of assessment tools the more likely that challenges will arise, if the most suitable ones are not used. This means that teachers need to take into consideration the ease of administering the test and the extent to which it reflects learners' learning.

Evidence from literature shows that in any of the assessment tools, three interconnected elements which fall in what Pellegrino (2014) called the assessment triangle. Pellegrino (2014) asserts that prior to adopting an assessment tool, three things need to be considered. The first is students' cognition (i.e. how they acquire knowledge and understanding of a subject). The second is the assumption that the assessment will provide evidence of students' competence. The third is the way in which teachers interpret the evidence. This model of assessment provides a useful framework for analyzing and determining how well the learning goals have been accomplished and for designing future valid assessments tools (Pellegrino & Hickey, 2006). Notable fact across each of the three elements is that they must have a meaningful connection to each other to ensure valid and sound inferences about students' learning outcomes.

4 Conclusion

This chapter has answered the question, "*What makes the 21st-century teacher different from previous centuries' teachers in terms of knowledge and skills?*" The answer was informed by assessing what was important for teachers to be effective in preparing students for the 21st-century. Three important factors were unfolded: These include; effective pedagogical and assessment practices and role of professional ethics and values. Based on our review and the theories and models used, we conclude that gone are the days when learning is curriculum centered because now teachers must not only teach the content but also provide students with the skills that will enable them to use the knowledge they have acquired beyond the classroom setting. In this regard, teachers' ability to use ICT is very important, as the Fourth Industrial Revolution requires people to be computer literate. This means that since knowledge acquisition has become digitalized and jobs are rapidly changing, teachers are supposed to be lifelong learners to enable their students to become marketable in the labor market. This will ultimately enable them to integrate the content, pedagogy and technology to acquire the skills appropriate for their for the 21st century.

Teachers also need to apply innovative teaching and assessment approaches that personalize learning while ensuring students are motivated to learn. Lastly, teachers should embrace character building as an integral part of education. Students' behavior, attitudes, morals and values need to be equally emphasized along with acquiring relevant knowledge prior to joining the 21st-century world of work. Besides, this cannot be possible if teachers themselves do not own and see the value and meaning of these skills due to lack of knowledge. Therefore, teacher training institutions need to integrate moral and ethical issues in the curriculum to ensure that trainee teachers understand their importance. Also, ongoing professional support is vital to enable teachers to become lifelong learners and so learning how to learn should be part and parcel of our education system in the 21st century.

References

Anangisye, W. A. L. (2010). Promoting teacher ethics in colleges of teacher education in Tanzania: Practices and challenges. *African Journal of Teacher Education, 1*(1), 64–77.

Anangisye, W. A. L. (2011). Why are teachers motivated to behave unprofessionally? A qualitative-data-based-inquiry on educational stakeholders' experiences in Tanzania. *A Journal of Contemporary Research, 8*(1), 1–23.

Anderson, C., & Palm, T. (2017). Characteristics of improved formative assessment practice. *Education Inquiry, 8*(2), 104–122. https://doi.org/10.1080/20004508.2016.1275185

American Association of Colleges of Teacher Education (AACTE) Committee on Innovation and Technology. (2008). *Handbook of Technological Pedagogical Content Knowledge (TPCK) for educators*. Routledge.

Binkley, M., Erstad, O., Herman, J., Raizen, S., Ripley, M., Miller-Ricci, M., & Rumble, M. (2010). Defining 21st century skills. In E. Care, P. Griffin, & B. McGaw (Eds.), *Assessment and teaching of 21st century skills* (pp. 17–66). Springer.

Black, P., & Wiliam, D. (2009). Developing the theory of formative assessment. *Educational Assessment, Evaluation and Accountability, 21*(1), 5–31.

Blömeke, S., Gustafsson, J.-E., & Shavelson, R. (2015). Beyond dichotomies, competence viewed as a continuum. *Zeitschrift für Psychologie, 223*, 3–13. doi:10.1027/2151-2604/a000194

Care, E. (2018). 21st century skills: From theory to action. In E. Care, P. Griffin, & M. Wilson (Eds.), *Assessment and teaching of 21st century skills: Research and applications* (pp. 3–17). Springer.

Care, E., Kim, H., Vista, A., & Anderson, K. (2018). *Education system alignment for 21st century skills: Focus on assessment*. Center for Universal Education, Brookings Institution.

Chalkiadaki, A. (2018). A systematic literature review of the 21st century skills and competences in primary education. *International Journal of Instruction, 11*(3), 1–16.

Chowdhury, M. (2016). Emphasizing morals, values, ethics, and character education in science education and science teaching. *The Malaysian Online Journal of Educational Science, 4*(2), 2–16.

Chu, S. K. W., Reynolds, R. B., Tavares, N. J. Notari, M., & Lee, C. W. Y. (2017). Assessment instruments for twenty-first century skills. In S. Chu, R. Reynolds, M. Notari, N. Taveres, & C. Lee (Eds.), *21st century skills development through inquiry based learning from theory to practice* (pp. 163–192). Springer Science.

Daisy, D. (2015). Teachers' conduct in the 21st century: The need for enhancing students' academic performance. *Journal of Education and Practice, 6*(35), 71–78.

Darling-Hammond, L., & Pecheone, R. (2009). Reframing accountability: Using performance assessments to focus learning on higher-order skills. In L. M. Pinkus (Ed.), *Meaningful measurement: The role of assessments in improving high school education in the twenty-first century*. Alliance for Excellent Education.

Dewey, J. (1929). *The quest for certainty*. Minton.

Driscoll, M. (2000). *Psychology of learning for instruction*. Allyn & Bacon.

Fussy, D. S. (2018). Institutionalization of teacher ethics in secondary schools: A school heads' perspective. *Pakistan Journal of Education, 32*(2), 79–96.

Gable, R. A., Hendrickson, J. M., Tonelson, S. W., & Van Acker, R. (2000). Changing disciplinary and instructional practices in the middle school to address IDEA. *The Clearing House, 73*(4), 205–208.

Gotch, C., & French, B. (2014). A systematic review of assessment literacy measures. *Educational Measurement: Issues and Practice, 33*(2), 14–18.

Gulikers, J. T. M., Bastiaens, T. J., & Kirschner, P. A. (2004). A five-dimensional framework for authentic assessment. *Educational Technology Research and Development, 52*, 67–86.

Hameed, S. A. (2011). Effect of internet drawbacks on moral and social values of users in education. *Australian Journal of Basic and Applied Sciences, 5*(6), 372–380.

Isaacs, T., Zara, C., Herbert, G., Coombs, S. J., & Smith, C. (2013). *Key concepts in educational assessment*. Sage Publications Ltd.

Kolb, D. A. (1984). *Experiential learning: Experience as a source of learning and development*. Prentice-Hall.

Kozma, B. B. (2011). ICT, educational transformation and economic development: An analysis of the US national education technology plan. *E-learning and Digital Media, 8*(2), 106–120. https://doi.org/10.2304/elea.2011.8.2.106

Lawrence-Brown, D. (2004). Differentiated instruction: Inclusive strategies for standards-based learning that benefit the whole class. *American Secondary Education, 32*(3), 34–62.

Lemke, C., Coughlin, E., Thadani, V., & Martin, C. (2003). *enGauge 21st century skills. Literacy in the digital age*. NCRL/Metiri Group. Retrieved January 11, 2020, from http://www.metiri.com/features.html

Mishra, P., & Koehler, M. J. (2006). Technological pedagogical content knowledge: A framework for integrating technology in teachers' knowledge. *Teachers College Record, 108*(6), 1017–1054.

Mdemu, A. Z. (2013). *Teachers' perceptions of their roles as moral educators in Tanzania: A study of selected secondary schools in Iringa Municipality*. Unpublished Master Dissertation, University of Dar es Salaam.

Ministry of Education and Vocational Training [MoEVT]. (2010). *Education sector development program: Secondary education development program II*. MoEVT.

Mkimbili, S., & Kitta, S. K. (2019). The rationale of continuous assessment for development of competencies in Tanzania secondary schools. *Advanced Journal of Social Science, 6*(1), 64–70. https://doi.org/10.21467/ajss.6.1.64-70

National Institute of Education [NIE]. (2009). *A teacher education model for the 21st century: A report by the National Institute of Education, Singapore*. Retrieved March 14, 2020, from http://www.nie.edu.sg/files/TE21%20online%20version%20-%20updated.pdf

Okobaa, V. (2017). Preparing the teacher to meet the challenges of a changing world. *Journal of Education and Practice, 8*(5), 81–86.

Olusegun, B. S. (2015). Constructivism learning theory: A paradigm for teaching and learning. *IOSR Journal of Research & Method in Education (IOSR-JRME), 5*(6), 66–70.

Organisation for Economic Co-Operation and Development [OECD]. (2005). *The definition and selection of key competencies* (Executive summary). Retrieved December 10, 2019, from http://www.oecd.org/dataoecd/47/61/35070367.pdf

Palm, T. (2008). Performance assessment and authentic assessment: A conceptual analysis of the literature. *Practical Assessment, Research & Evaluation, 13*(4), 1–11.

Paulo, A., & Tilya, F. (2014). The 2005 secondary school curriculum reforms in Tanzania: Disjunction between policy and practice in its implementation. *Journal of Education and Practice, 5*(35), 114–122.

Pellegrino, J. W. (2014). Assessment as a positive influence on 21st century teaching and learning: A systems approach to progress. *Psicología Educativa, 20*, 65–77.

Pellegrino, J. W., & Hickey, D. (2006). Educational assessment: Towards better alignment between theory and practice. In L. Verschaffel, F. Dochy, M. Boekaerts, & S. Vosniadou (Eds.), *Instructional psychology: Past, present and future trends. Sixteen essays in honour of Erik De Corte* (pp. 169–189). Elsevier.

Piaget, J. (1980). The psychogenesis of knowledge and its epistemological significance. In M. Piatelli-Palmarini (Ed.), *Language and learning* (pp. 23–34). Harvard University Press.

Price, J. K., Pierson, E., & Light, D. (2011). *Using classroom assessment to promote 21st century learning in emerging market countries*. Paper presented at Global Learn Asia Pacific, Melbourne Australia.

Rasheed, F., & Wahid, A. (2018). The theory of differentiated instruction and its applicability: An e-learning perspective. *International Journal of Technical & Non-Technical Research, IX*(IV), 193–202.

Richards, J. C., & Schmidt, R. (2002). *Longman dictionary of language teaching and applied linguistics*. Pearson Education.

Schaeffer, E. (1999). It's time for schools to implement character education. *NASSP Bulletin, 83*, 1–7.

Schleicher, A. (Ed.). (2012). *Preparing teachers and developing school leaders for the 21st century: Lessons from around the world*. OECD Publishing.

Schmidt-Crawford, D. A., Thompson, A. D., Baran, E., Mishra, P., Koehler, M. J., & Shin, T. S. (2009). Technological Pedagogical Content Knowledge (TPACK): The development and validation of an assessment instrument for preservice teachers. *Journal of Research on Technology in Education, 4*(2), 123–149.

Sherpa, K. (2018). Importance of professional ethics for teachers. *International Educational and Research Journal, 4*(3), 16–18.

Sirotnik, K. A. (1990). Society, schooling, teaching, and preparing to teach. In J. I. Goodlad, R. Soder, & K. A. Sirotnik (Eds.), *The moral dimensions of teaching* (pp. 296–327). Jossey-Bass Publishers.

Stewart, D. W., & Kamins, M. A. (Eds.). (1993). *Secondary research: Information sources and methods*. Sage. https://dx.doi.org/10.4135/9781412985802

Subban, P. (2006). Differentiated instruction: A research basis. *International Education Journal, 7*(7), 935–947.

Thompson, A., & Mishra, P. (2007). Breaking news: TPCK becomes TPACK! *Journal of Computing in Teacher Education, 24*(2), 38–64.

Tomlinson, C. A. (2005). Grading and differentiation: Paradox or good practice? *Theory into Practice, 44*(3), 262–269.

Türkkahraman, M. (2012). The role of education in the societal development. *Journal of Educational and Instructional Studies in the World, 2*(4), 38–41.

UNESCO. (2017). *Education for sustainable development goals: Learning objectives.* UNESCO. https://unesdoc.unesco.org/ark:/48223/pf0000247444

United Nations Educational, Scientific and Cultural Organization. (2008a). *ICT competency standards for teachers. Implementation guidelines.* Retrieved December 10, 2019, from http://unesdoc.unesco.org/images/0015/001562/156209e.pdf

United Nations Educational, Scientific and Cultural Organization. (2008b). *ICT competency standards for teachers. Policy framework.* Retrieved December, 2019, from http://unesdoc.unesco.org/images/0015/001562/156210e.pdf

United Nations Educational, Scientific and Cultural Organization [UNESCO]. (2015). *2013 Asia-Pacific Education Research Institutes Network (ERI-Net) regional study on transversal competencies in education policy & practice (phase 1).* UNESCO.

VanTassel-Baska, J. (2013). Performance-based assessment: The road to authentic learning for the gifted. *Gifted Child Today, 37*(1), 41–47.

Vaughn, S., Bos, C., & Schumm, J. (2000). *Teaching exceptional, diverse, and at-risk students in the general education classroom* (2nd ed.). Allyn and Bacon.

Vlachou, M. A. (2018). Classroom assessment practices in middle school science lessons: A study among Greek science teachers. *Cogent Education, 5,* 1–19. https://doi.org/10.1080/2331186X.2018.1455633

Voogt, J., & Roblin, N. P. (2012). A comparative analysis of international frameworks for 21st century competences: Implications for national curriculum policies. *Journal of Curriculum Studies, 44*(3) 299–321.

Vygotskiĭ, L. S. (1962). *Thought and language.* MIT Press.

Yousefpoori-Naeim, M. (2014). Performance-based assessment: What we should know about it? *ROSHD FLT Journal, 29*(2), 39–47. https://www.academia.edu/25306558/Performance_Based_Assessment_What_We_Should_Know_about_It

CHAPTER 7

Pre-Service Technology Teachers' Learning Experiences of Teaching Methods for Integrating the Use of Technologies for the Fourth Industrial Revolution

Asheena Singh-Pillay

Abstract

One of the challenges teacher educators face today is the need to integrate learning technologies into the learning experiences of pre-service teachers to equip them with innovative and responsive teaching methods to be able to teach in the Fourth Industrial Revolution. These responsive teaching methods will equip them to address and solve contextual problems faced by society and develop 21st-century skills. Case studies are a responsive teaching method that was embraced in the teaching of a technology education module. These case studies required pre-service teachers to use the Internet of Things, to equip them to be able to teach in the Fourth Industrial Revolution. The current chapter focuses on pre-service technology teachers' learning experiences of using the Internet of Things when engaging in case studies to solve local contextual problems. There is a paucity of research on pre-service teachers' learning experiences of teaching methods integrating the use of the Internet of Things in developing countries like South Africa. Hence the need for this study. Data was generated via reflective journals and focus group interviews from 18 pre-service teachers. Informed consent of pre-service teachers was sought, and they were assured of confidentiality and anonymity. Focus group interviews were audio-recorded and were transcribed verbatim. Thereafter transcripts were sent to participants for member checking, to ensure that the recordings were an accurate representation of what they meant to say. The findings revealed that pre-service technology teachers engaged in deep and surface approaches to learning when they used the Internet of Things, they encountered learning experiences regarding their teacher agency. They valued and enjoyed case studies that targeted to resolve contextual issues. These findings have implications for the kinds of tasks that are designed to prepare pre-service teachers to teach in the Fourth Industrial Revolution within an African context.

1   Introduction

The teaching and learning environment is no longer confined to 'chalk and talk' as it has been revolutionized by emerging technologies such as artificial intelligence (AI), robotics, the Internet of Things (IoT), autonomous vehicles, 3-D printing, nanotechnology, biotechnology, materials science, energy storage, and quantum computing (Morrar, Arman, & Mousa, 2017). Technology has become a quintessential component in a teachers' toolkit of pedagogies. This means that education and the use of technologies in education are intrinsically connected and cannot be separated. The effective use of teaching technologies has made it possible for enhancing students' engagement with the course material, ensuring students' progress as active learners by structuring information mentally, improving visualization, encouraging independence of students as well as improving social interaction of students (de Ruyter, Brown, & Burgess, 2019).

Based on the aforementioned points, it stands to reason that technology is not just a gadget or tool to be used in isolation within the classroom to improve or benefit the teaching and learning of content only. Rather it is a socially embedded medium that shapes our daily existence and experiences, for example, wheelbarrows, tractors, cell phones, trains, and aeroplanes were developed in response to society's needs and they impact our lives and experiences daily. Certain technologies, for example, the Internet of Things, robots and 3-D printers have a dual purpose whereby they could be used during teaching and learning to develop 21st-century skills among students such as critical thinking, problem-solving, creativity, people management, coordinating with others, emotional intelligence, decision-making, cognitive flexibility, responsible citizenship and agency as well as a vehicle to address and solve many contextual problems that communities encounter. This means that communities can benefit when students use technologies to solve contextual problems in case studies.

I am aware of the debate put forth by Lelliot, Pendlebury, and Enslin (2001) who warn that the social embeddedness of technology leads to an unavoidable dilemma in Africa and that access to technology (or a lack thereof) will bring new forms of exclusion which could lead to more poverty and social ills. However, I argue that if the technology is used appropriately during teaching and learning, it can be used for social innovation to address contextual challenges in the local community (Allenby & Sarewitz, 2011). This means that technologies can be used to meet social needs and tackle social challenges (Marolt Pucihar & Zimmermann, 2015). For technologies to be used within the teaching and learning environment for social innovation and as leverage to address socio-economic challenges, teaching and learning activities must be well-structured to include technology-based learning activities that address societal challenges. Put simply this means that in well-structured lessons, on the one hand technology could bridge the dichotomy that often exists between theory and application of theory in practice to solve contextual problems in society. While on the other hand, it could illuminate how communities benefit via their indirect access to technologies when it is used for social innovation during teaching to address contextual challenges. One such technology that can be used during teaching and learning to address societal challenges is the Internet of Things (IoT). The IoT is a networked world of connected devices, objects, and people that is responsive to the needs of individuals and society as it was created to make life and business easy (Greengard, 2015). This chapter assumes the position that curriculum development and the practice of teaching and learning should be aligned to the needs of the communities they serve.

In the teaching of technology education opportunities to engage students in the application of theory to solve contextual problems in society occur via the design process, capability task, resource task, and case studies. Case study tasks were used in this study to solve contextual problems which will be elaborated upon under the case study section. This chapter reports on practice-led research which highlights how technologies can be used in case study activities in a socially responsive way to address real contextual problems and further exposes Pre-service Technology teachers' (PSTTs) learning experiences of teaching methods using the Internet of Things to address real contextual problems.

2   Case Study Activities in Technology Education

In technology education, case studies are usually short, structured tasks. Their purpose is to link real-life examples of technological challenges in society to classroom activities. Case studies help to find solutions to contextual problems and allow for reflection about learning, responsible citizenship, agency, problem-solving, creativity, design, and appropriateness of the solution provided (DBE, 2011). Case study tasks include the use of simulations, observations, interviews, and the Internet of Things (IoT). The IoT uses smart devices and the Internet to provide innovative solutions to various challenges and issues in society (Kumar, Tiwari, & Zylmber, 2019). It links the objects of the real world with the virtual world, thus enabling anytime, anywhere connectivity for anything and anyone (Dwivedi, Janssen, Slade, Rana, Weerakkody, Millard, & Snijders, 2017). In other words, the IoT refers to a world where physical objects and beings, as well as virtual data and environments, all interact with each other by exchanging data and information gathered about the environment while reacting to the triggers of the physical world with the ability to influence ongoing processes with their actions (Santucci, 2010).

Most case study assignments require students to answer an open-ended question or develop a solution to an open-ended problem with multiple potential solutions. Case study assignments can be done individually or in teams so that students can brainstorm solutions and share the workload. Most case studies have these common elements: (i) a question or problem that needs to be solved; (ii) a description of the problem's context (a law, an industry, a family); and (iii) supporting data, which may include data tables, links to URLs, quoted statements or verification, supporting documents, audio, images or video (Dunne & Brooks, 2004).

I requested students to follow a systematic approach as suggested by Dunne and Brooks, (2004) to address the case study. For example:
- What is the issue?
- What is the context of the problem?
- What key facts should be considered?
- What alternatives are available to the decision-maker?
- What would you recommend and why?

2.1   Task

Students were expected to design and build a wireless watering system to remotely irrigate a small garden or farm in a rural community. Table 7.1 summarizes the common elements of the case study teaching method for the case assignment.

TABLE 7.1   Common elements of the case study for teaching method

Elements	Participant	Task/comment
Decision-maker	Lecturer	Presented the wireless network module.
Problem description	Lecturer and PSTTS	To design and build a wireless watering system to remotely irrigate a small garden or farm in a rural community.
Supporting data	Lecturer, PSTTS and laboratory technician	Course content, the use of the Internet and the apparatus provided by the laboratory technician.

3 Methodology

As the objective of this study was to explore PSTTs' learning experiences of teaching methods using the IoT to address real contextual problems, a qualitative approach was adopted. Qualitative research aims to understand and explore the phenomenon, namely the learning experiences of PSTTs of teaching methods using IoT to address contextual problems, from the perspective of the participants (Cohen, Manion, & Morrison, 2017). The interpretative paradigm was embraced in this study, to reveal the essence of the participants' learning experiences of using the Internet of things when engaging in case studies to solve local contextual problems from their perspectives (Henning, Van Rensburg, & Smit, 2004).

PSTTs (18) enrolled for the exit level technology education module were purposively selected to participate in this study. Informed consent of participants was sought, and they were assured of confidentiality and anonymity. All 18 PSTTs[1] consented to participate in this study. PSTTs were requested to self-select groups. Three groups with 6 PSTTs per group were formed. Each group was tasked with the case study assignment: to design and build an irrigation system using the IoT. This system could be an automated irrigation system or a mobile irrigation system. Students were requested to use Python Programming (https://www.python.org/) because it is easier to learn, allows system integration, and is recommended by literature as one of the relevant programming languages for the case studies (Schwab, 2017; Hariharasudan & Kot, 2018). The students organized different components, that is, microcontroller/processors, GSM module, moisture sensors, driver, relay, water pump, bread/circuit board and light-emitting diodes (LEDs) to conduct their case assignment.

Permission to conduct this study was acquired from Richwood University. Data was generated via interviews and reflective journals. The interview questions focused on the following issues: experiences of case study tasks in technology education, using the Internet of Things to address the case studies, working collaboratively with their colleagues and teacher agency. Interviews were audio-recorded and transcribed verbatim, and thereafter transcripts were sent to participants for member checking. According to Creswell and Creswell (2018), member checking enhances the credibility of the study. Member checking allows participants to read individual interview transcripts to ensure data was captured correctly on the phenomenon being explored, and to avoid misinterpretation by the researcher due to the possibility of mishearing what had been said.

Data were analyzed using content analysis which involved the organization of the data into categories (Ezzy, 2002). In the study, coding was used to categorize the data that had been collected. Coding is the process of identifying concepts or themes that are in the data (Ezzy, 2002), which involves noting regularities in the setting or participants chosen for the study (De Vos, 2004). To begin the coding process, the author read all the transcripts and identified initial themes established from the data. The assigned themes were analyzed and coded more closely. Using a continuous comparative method of analysis (Corbin & Strauss, 2008), the author analyzed all transcripts and explored patterns or dissimilarities in the data, and identified themes as they emerged through an interpretative lens.

4   Findings and Discussion

In this section, data from the interviews and reflective journals are presented to bring to the fore PSTTs' learning experiences to teaching methods using the Internet of Things to address real contextual problems. Four themes emerged, PSTTs approaches to learning, PSTTs learning experiences of case study learning using IoT, PSTTs learning experience of teacher agency, and PSTTs learning experiences of social learning.

4.1   *PSTTs' Approaches to Learning Using IoT in Case Study Projects*

The data from the reflective journal and interviews reveal that PSTTs embraced deep and surface approaches to learning when using the IoT during their case study task. First, the deep approaches to learning will be presented followed by the surface approaches to learning. On the one hand, the majority of (13) PSTTs viewed learning through the IoT as a way to improve understanding of wireless networks and irrigation systems to develop a broader and deeper perspective on the case study by being able to explore and evaluate information from multiple sites in a short space of time. The excerpts below reflect the in-depth learning approach used by PSTTs.

> The Internet as a technological tool for research has widened my ability of reading, sifting information, comparing information, synthesizing information needed to develop the remote-controlled irrigation system. I feel I am also able to process and make sense of all the information I have, I combine it to information from the Internet with that obtained in lectures and contained in the course pack. (PSTT: 6, Reflective journal)
>
> I do not need to depend on one source when utilizing the Internet like I would have had to if I were to use a book, I just move from one source to another, comparing contrasting and at the end, select the best, accurate

and suitable source to construct the wireless irrigation system. (PSTT: 9, Interview)

The above excerpts highlight how PSTTs used the IoT to enhance their discerning abilities, by comparing, sifting, contrasting and synthesizing information available to them. The above approaches reported by PSTTs reveal that they engage with the information source, evaluate the information and integrate it with information from their lectures and course pack. This means that the IoT was used as a way of learning through integration, analysis, evaluation with a focus on the possibility to assess the accuracy of the facts by cross-checking them. The above-mentioned approach of checking and cross-checking has resulted in a broader scope of interpretation, reading for meaning, and learning. The approaches reported in the preceding excerpts describe deeper approaches to critically integrating sources of information with a focus on analyzing and evaluating resources to resolve a contextual problem (building an irrigation system). Key strategies involved summarizing, comparing, critiquing, and synthesizing ideas. The above finding concurs with that of Rohman, Fauzan, and Yohandri (2020) study which illuminates the 21st-century skills, such as critical thinking, problem-solving, analyzing, comparing, contrasting that learners develop when they engage in projects that depend on the use of digital technologies.

On the other hand, a few (5) PSTTs engaged in a more surface approach to learning when using the IoT as is visible in the excerpts below:

> I surf the net to collect information, copy and paste and find an easy solution for the case study it just to meet the requirement, it is an opportunity to go on Twitter, Facebook, Instagram. (PSTT: 11, Reflective journal)

> I spend a minimum of time copying and pasting information for the project so that I can have more time for entertainment and social networking. (PSTT: 4, Interview)

From the above excerpts, it is visible that these PSTTs spend more time on the IoT for social networking rather than their case study task; hence they focused mainly on combining rather than interrogating sources of information related to the case study task. A key feature of the more surface approaches to learning using the Internet focused mostly around collecting and replicating information. The visible strategy of these approaches reported by PSTTs was the indiscriminate tendency to copy and paste, with no effort to interrogate, compare, analyze or synthesize information. Further, they emphasized the need to find an easy solution for the case study task to meet class requirements. The above finding resonates with that of Schindler, Burkholder, Morad, and Marchs' (2017) study on students' learning patterns in higher education and beyond. The study reported that 30 percent of students who use the IoT for learning spend more time on social media and engage in surface learning patterns.

4.2   PSTTS' Learning Experiences of Case Study Learning Using IoT

Data from the reflective journals and the interviews illuminate that PSTTs foregrounded the benefits of the Internet of Things in solving case studies that focus on contextual problems as is evident in the excerpts below:

> I'm starting to realize how easily the IoT can be used to improve the quality of our lives, I could apply the theory learned to solve the real practical problem encountered in my community for example women could be assisted to control the timer on the stove from their phone so that when they get home meals are ready and they can spend time with their children. The IoT allows us to live smartly, all assessment tasks should require us to use IoT to solve problems experienced in our communities, I enjoy tasks of this nature where we have to solve contextual problems. (PSTT: 7, Reflective journal)

Comments made by the PSTTs in the interview seem to concur with the comments received in the reflective journal.

> The IoT is beneficial to the rural farmers, it allowed them to enhance productivity and reduce the time spent on watering their garden, we must be exposed to more of this type of task it helps us to apply theory learned to solve real contextual problems affecting people in our community that is what learning and teaching should be about. (PSTT: 18, Interview)

From the above excerpts, it is evident that PSTTs enjoyed working on the case study task using the IoT as it allowed them the space to apply the theory learned to solve contextual problems. The case study assessment task provided opportunities for PSTTs to transform their learning experiences by engaging them in contextually relevant projects. In traditional learning environments, attention to the context in which learning takes place as well as the interaction between learners and the surrounding environment is often neglected or ignored (Darling-Hammond, Flook, Cook-Harvey, Barron, & Osher, 2020). In this instance, case study tasks ensured continuity of the learning experience (apply theory to solve the real problems) by promoting opportunities to practice and apply content and skills learned in lectures to solve real contextual problems. In case study tasks, real contexts are brought into the classroom, and thus the contexts are meaningful and concrete to the learner. According to Lindsay (2017), the more personalized and relevant the tasks are to students' daily lives and aimed at addressing societal issues in their communities, the more invested they become in finding appropriate solutions and carrying out the task. The above finding is aligned with that of Mok (2017) who established IoT tasks that motivate students to engage with difficult content and apply theory to solve practical problems encountered in society.

PSTTs acknowledge that the IoT is a useful technological resource that can be used to solve contextual problems in their communities. They realize the social embeddedness of IoT and its positive impact on addressing contextual issues and challenges such as assisting working people, health benefits, and saving time in the above excerpts.

4.3   *PSTTs' Learning Experiences of Teacher Agency*

By engaging in case study tasks, PSTTs had multiple opportunities for deeper inner reflection. The data from both the reflective journal and interviews reveal that case study tasks using the IoT catalyze PSTTs' awareness of their role as agents of change. Reflections allowed 18 PSTTs to (re)evaluate their frame of reference regarding what a teacher's job is and what it is not as is visible in the excerpts that follow:

> If it weren't for this task, I would have ignored the using IoT and trying to solve the problem encountered in communities. To me, I was supposed to learn about sensors, interfacing them and connectivity, write the exams and pass. Helping to solve community issues, driving change is not my job, my job will be just to teach, now I feel differently, I have changed it's not just about passing it's also about my learning as a lifelong learner, I have changed because of this case study task, my thinking about me as a teacher and my role in the community has changed, I can use my teacher voice to change people's lives, improve our society, it's my responsibility, I now care about my community. (PSTT: 15, Reflective journal)

Likewise, excerpts from the interviews support the views expressed in the reflective journal:

> I know now that change can be little steps we take to improve the quality of life for others in our community, it doesn't have to be grand and fancy. Working on this project let me see that I can contribute to change. Even

though this project was on a wireless irrigation system, I found I could not ignore other challenges the community encounters, I took it upon myself to tell the working mother on how to control her washing machine and oven from her cell phone to make her life a little easier. I felt inspired and would want to do this type of project again. I will engage my learners in this type of project when I start teaching, this is real contextualized learning. (PSTT: 16, Interview)

The above excerpts highlight the transformative learning that occurs by engaging PSTTs in contextualized case study tasks using the IoT. By using the community as a resource, PSTTs had an opportunity to (re)align their frames of references. The consequence of the realignment of their frame of reference was a transition from ignorance of the social responsibilities attached to teaching (it not my job) to a greater sense of awareness of the need to bring about change, transformation and social justice in the communities they are working in (this is my responsibility; I can make a difference). The case study tasks allowed PSTTs to be conscious of their roles as agents of change in the communities they worked in; they became aware of power or social capital (teacher's voice), inequalities that prevail, and their civic responsibility towards the community. PSTTs can see how their role as an agent of change extends from the school classroom to the community. These PSTTs were able to see the power linked to the professional identity of a teacher and the capacity to produce change. These participants see teaching as a moral-ethical value-laden practice. Powers (2004), in her evaluation of school community case study projects in the United States, found that this approach increases students' interest in their community issues. These findings confirm that the use of a case study approach to address contextual issues makes a difference in how PSTTs view their role as agents of change. Contextualized case study tasks led to caring PSTTs who reflected upon their communities' challenges (Orr, 1992; Theobald, 2000) during case studies.

4.4 *PSTTs' Learning Experiences of Social Learning When Using the IoT during Case Studies*

Case study tasks using the IoT provided PSTTs with reflective spaces to question, (re)examine their (un)conscious values, beliefs, and judgments in life as is visible in the excerpts below:

> I don't like working in groups but in this case study project, I had a chance to collaborate with people in my group, I normally don't speak to them, we are faces in the same lecture room. They treated me kindly, were so warm towards me. The best part was I learned how to be a team player,

not to be judgemental, trust the judgment of others and be confident, this was a humbling experience for me. I gained more skills during this project than passing any exam. (PSTT: 17, Reflective journal)

I realized problem-solving becomes easier and solutions are reached faster when we work together. I am independent I work by myself, in this project I learned about group dynamics, trust, to listen to other voice, to share ideas, I learned about teamwork, strengths and weakness and how to help and be helped. (PSTT: 2, Interview)

The excerpts above confirm that case study tasks using the IoT allow for collaborative reciprocal learning, promote deep thinking about actions, help to break stereotypes and allow PSTTs to believe in the good of others. The reflective space that case study tasks provided helped PSTTs to gain a better understanding of themselves (be a team player).

PSTTs' engagement in case study tasks using the IoT helped them to break down stereotypes, produced positive feelings toward group members and developed collegial relationships. In a way, the reflection processes attached to the task were liberating as it provided PSTTs with the skills needed to successfully manage life tasks such as identifying anxieties, labelling emotions, learning in groups, teamwork, awareness of themselves and others, the need for kindness and respect for others, forming relationships, caring about others, making good decisions, behaving ethically, avoiding negative behavior and overcoming biases which Zins, Weissberg, Wang, and Walberg (2004) refer to as emotional learning. The emotional catharsis that PSTTs experienced during the case study tasks is important as they are a part of what concerns education (Sen, 2009) as they bring to the fore the humanistic dimension of teaching and learning as well as important emotional competencies pre-service teachers need to be able to relate to each other and their learners in future.

5 Conclusion

The findings of this study revealed that the majority of PSTTs engaged in deep approaches to learning when using the IoT, they read critically, compared, analyzed, synthesized, and evaluated information accessed from the Internet and compared the information retrieved to information obtained via lectures and the course pack. A few PSTTs resorted to surface approaches to learning when using the IoT, they copied and pasted information and completed the case study to meet the requirements for the module. PSTTs enjoyed working on the case study tasks using the IoT as a teaching method as it allowed them the space to apply the theory learned to solve contextual problems. Engaging with the case study tasks enhanced PSTTs' learning experience of teacher agency as well as their learning experiences of social learning. The above findings support the initial argument made in this chapter if the technology is used appropriately during teaching and learning, it can be used for social innovation to address contextual challenges in the local community. In other words, the findings of this study elucidate that when teaching and learning activities are well designed, technologies associated with the Fourth Industrial Revolution can be used to develop 21st-century skills among PSTTs while addressing contextual social challenges.

Note

1 PSTTs were coded from 1–18, for example PSTT 13 refers to the participant coded as 13 and so on.

References

Allenby, B. R., & Sarew, D. (2011). *The techno-human condition*. The MIT Press.
Cohen, L., Manion, L., & Morrison, K. (2017). *Research methods in education*. Routledge Taylor and Francis Group.
Corbin, J., & Strauss, A. (2008). *Basics of qualitative research: Techniques and procedures for developing grounded theory* (3rd ed.). Sage Publications, Inc.
Creswell, J. W., & Creswell, J. D. (2017). *Research design: Qualitative, quantitative, and mixed methods approaches*. Sage Publications.
de Ruyter, A., Brown, M., & Burgess, J. (2019). GIG work and the Fourth Industrial Revolution. *Journal of International Affairs, 72*(1), 37–50. https://www.jstor.org/stable/10.2307/26588341
Darling-Hammond, L., Flook, L., Cook-Harvey, C., Barron, B., & Osher, D. (2020). Implications for educational practice of the science of learning and development. *Applied Developmental Science, 24*(2), 97–140. doi:10.1080/10888691.2018.1537791
Department of Basic Education. (2011). *Curriculum assessment policy statement – grade 7–9-technology education*. Pretoria.
De Vos, A. S. (2004). Combined quantitative and qualitative approach. In A. S. De Vos, H. Strydom, C. B. Fouché, & C. S. L. Delport (Eds.), *Research at grassroots for the social sciences and human service professions* (2nd ed.). Van Schaik Publishers.
Dunne, D., & Brooks, K. (2004). *STLHE Green guide no. 5: Teaching with cases*. http://www.mcmaster.ca/stlhe/publications/gree.guides.htm
Dwivedi, Y. K., Janssen, M., Slade, E. L., Rana, N. P., Weerakkody, V., Millard, J., & Snijders, D. (2017). Driving innovation through Big Open Linked Data (BOLD): Exploring

antecedents using interpretive structural modelling. *Information Systems Frontiers, 19*(2), 197–212. https://doi.org/10.1007/s10796-016-9675-5

Ezzy, D. (2002). *Qualitative analysis: Practice and innovation*. Allen & Unwin.

Greengard, S. (2015). *The Internet of Things*. MIT Press.

Hariharasudan, A., & Kot, S. (2018). A scoping review on digital english and education 4.0 for industry 4.0. *Social Sciences, 7*(11), 22–240.

Henning, E., Van Rensburg, W., & Smit, B. (2004). *Finding your way in qualitative research*. Van Schaik Publishers.

Kumar, S., Tiwari, P., & Zylmber, M. (2019). Internet of Things is a revolutionary approach for future technology enhancement: A review. *Journal of Big Data, 6,* 1–21. https://doi.org/10.1186/s40537-019-0268-2

Lelliott, A., Pendlebury, S., & Enslin, P. (2001). Online education in Africa: Promises and pitfalls. *South African Journal of Information Management, 3*(1), 1–10.

Lindsay, K. (2017). *Why IoT and personalization are made for each other*. CMS Wire.

Marolt, M., Pucihar, A., & Zimmermann, D. H. (2015). Social CRM adoption and its impact on performance outcomes: A literature review. *Organizacija, 48*(4), 260–271. http://doi.org/10.1515/orga-2015-0022

Mok, K. (2017). *Prototype: A smartphone universal remote for the Internet of Things*. The New Stack.

Morrar, R., Arman, H., & Mousa, S. (2017). The Fourth Industrial Revolution (Industry 4.0): A social innovation perspective. *Technology Innovation Management Review, 7*(11), 12–20. http://doi.org/10.22215/timreview/1117

Orr, D. (1992). *Ecological literacy education and transition to a post-modern world*. Albany State University of New York Press.

Powers, A. L. (2004). An evaluation of four place-based education programs. *The Journal of Environmental Education, 35*(4), 17–32.

Rohman, F., Fauzan, A., & Yohandri, Y. (2020). Project, Technology and Active (PROTECTIVE) learning model to develop digital literacy skills in the 21st century. *International Journal of Scientific & Technology Research, 9*(1), 12–16.

Santucci, G. (2010). *The internet of things: Between the revolution of the internet and the metamorphosis of objects*. Forum American Bar Association.

Schindler, L. A., Burkholder, G. J., Morad, O. A., & March, C. (2017). Computer-based technology and student engagement: A critical review of the literature. *International Journal of Educational Technology in High Education, 14*(25), 1–28. doi:10.1186/s41239-017-0063-0

Schwab, K. (2017). *The Fourth Industrial Revolution*. Crown Publishing Group.

Sen, A. (2009). *The idea of justice*. Allen Lane.

Theobald, P. (2000). Communities as curricula. *Forum for Applied Research and Public Policy, 15*(11), 106–111.

Zins, J. E., Weissberg, R. P., Wang, M. C., & Walberg, H. J. (Eds.). (2004). *Building academic success on social and emotional learning: What does the research say?* Teachers College Press.

CHAPTER 8

Pre-Service Teacher Educators' Experiences of Using Mobile Technologies in the Teaching and Learning of Mathematics and Technology Education for the Fourth Industrial Revolution

Asheena Singh-Pillay and Jayaluxmi Naidoo

Abstract

This qualitative ethnographic study reports on a project which sought to explore experiences of using mobile technologies, in the teaching and learning of mathematics and technology education. The researchers worked collaboratively to develop curricula featuring the use of mobile devices, in the context of their respective technology and mathematics education flipped lecture rooms, in response to the Fourth Industrial Revolution. Aligned with the module outcomes, mobile devices were used for teaching shapes, angles and design in mathematics and for applying the shapes, angles and design to build rigid structures in technology education. Mishra and Koehler's Technological, Pedagogical and Content Knowledge model undergirded this study. This chapter advances the rationale that teacher educators' pedagogical and technological practices cannot be understood without considering their socio-cultural backgrounds. The participants were teacher educators at one university in KwaZulu-Natal. Six teacher educators were purposively selected to participate in this study. Semi-structured interviews and observations were used to generate qualitative data. Data were subjected to content analysis. The findings reveal that teacher educators use mobile technologies to heighten students' awareness of mathematics and technology in everyday life, to initiate thinking by enabling students to move from the concrete, observable phenomena to abstract understanding of principles and their application to design to solve contextualized problems. Such use of mobile technologies enhances students' observation, discussion and presentation skills. Moreover, the findings highlight that teacher educators' pedagogy relating to mobile technologies are impacted by early learning experiences and socio-cultural background. The findings have implications for the Technological, Pedagogical and Content Knowledge model and calls for an extension of the model.

1 Introduction

Advances in technology influence the way people create, share, use and develop information in society. Nowadays computer devices are more powerful, easily accessible and come in a variety of forms, from those that are placed on our desks to those that are placed in the palm of our hands, for example, mobile devices. Mobile devices or technologies consist of portable two-way communications devices, namely, the computing device and the networking device that connects them. For this study, mobile technologies are used to refer to the use of mobile phones. The increasing variety and easy accessibility of technology have expanded the resources and the opportunities available to teachers to facilitate teaching and learning with technologies.

Furthermore, most students entering Higher Education are competent users of mobile phones and have excellent social networking skills acquired through experiential learning. Despite students' ability to use mobile phones and the potential to use mobile phones to facilitate the learning process, mobile technologies are not readily embraced during teaching in South African classrooms (Makoe, 2013; North, Johnston, & Ophoff, 2014; Ngesi, Landa, Madikiza, Cekiso, Tshotsho, & Walters, 2018). Also, Jita (2018) noted that not enough attention had been paid to the preparation of teachers to use technology tools for teaching. Similarly, Ekanayake and Wishart (2014) have pointed out that teacher training has been the least explored topic in mobile learning research. The points raised deep concerns among the researchers. Hence they explored the possibility of introducing teaching and learning with mobile devices during the teaching of mathematics and technology education, in a pre-service teacher education programme at a teacher training University in KwaZulu-Natal. This study responded to the following research question: What are pre-service teacher educators' experiences of using mobile technologies in the teaching and learning of mathematics and technology education?

It is envisaged that the introduction of teaching and learning with mobile devices will help to bridge the divide between theory and application of theory to solve the contextual problem as well as to prepare pre-service teachers to teach effectively with technologies in the Fourth Industrial Revolution (4IR). To embark on their research project, the researchers established the number of pre-service teachers enrolled for mathematics and technology education that have access to mobile phones (all pre-service teachers had smartphones). The researchers were aware that to use mobile phones to facilitate teaching and learning, there had to be a pedagogical focus. Hence, they designed their mathematics and technology education module outcomes, teaching strategies and learning tasks to integrate the use of mobile devices to teach shapes, angles and design in maths and application of shapes and angles to design rigid structures in technology education. Thus, this study sought to explore teacher educators' experiences of using mobile technologies in their pedagogical practice. This study aims to explain the connection between teacher educators' socio-cultural background, how they taught and how they used mobile phones in their teaching of shapes, angles and design in mathematics and the application of design in technology education.

The findings of this study can develop the implementation of an original intervention with mobile devices based on the results of the experiences of teacher educators and description of its affordances into a programme to bridge the gap between theory and the application of theory during problem-solving at a University in KwaZulu-Natal. Further, the findings of this study could create a platform for dialogue on the use of mobile devices research in pre-service teacher education programmes to prepare teachers for the Fourth Industrial Revolution.

2 Mobile Learning

Definitions of mobile learning emphasize mobility (Sharples, Arnedillo-Sánchez, Milrad, & Vavoula, 2009), access (Parsons & Ryu, 2006), immediacy (Kynäslahti, 2003), situativity (Cheon, Lee, Crooks, & Song, 2012), ubiquity (Kukulska-Hulme Sharples, Milrad, Arnedillo-Sánchez, & Vavoula, 2009), convenience (Kynäslahti, 2003), and context (Kearney, Schuck, Burden, & Aubusson, 2012). According to Sharples et al. (2009), mobile learning includes the characteristics of mobility in physical, conceptual, and social spaces. The relationship between the context of learning and context of being is unique to mobile learning, as learning may occur in independent, formal, or socialized contexts (Frohberg, Göth, & Schwabe, 2009).

Mobile learning (M-learning) embraces the use of mobile devices such as small wireless, portable, handheld devices (for example, cellular phones, smartphones, PDAS, MP3 players, portable game devices, tablets, notebooks and laptops), the capacity of human learning, social communication, interaction with the device, the learner and the societal aspects of learning (Kenny, Park, Van Neste-Kenny, Burton, & Meiers, 2009).

M-learning has the following benefits when the learning task is aligned with the learning outcome and teaching strategy, namely, it allows students to actively engage with the functions of mobile technology that allow for varying levels of interactivity and student-centeredness (Ozdamli & Cavus, 2011). The students learn by actively constructing, assimilating and applying new ideas and concepts based on both their previous and current knowledge; further, they take greater responsibility for their learning (Valk, Rashid, & Elder, 2010). These features provide opportunities for individualized, situated, collaborative, and informal learning without being limited to classroom contexts (Cheon, Lee, Crooks, & Song, 2012).

Despite the benefits of M-learning, it remains under-theorized in teacher education (Kearney & Maher, 2013), which emphasizes the need to inform teachers of the value of mobile technologies and how to integrate them effectively into their classes. Schuck, Aubusson, Kearney and Burden, (2013) and North, Johnston, and Ophoff (2014), noted that South African students predominantly use mobile phones for socializing, safety and privacy. Additionally, various reasons can be found in the literature about teachers' concerns about integrating mobile technologies in their teaching.

3   A Global Perspective on Mobile Learning

The popularity and acceptance of mobile learning are gaining momentum around the world due to the increasing availability of low-cost mobile devices and supporting infrastructure for mobile technology (Jalil, Beer, & Crowther, 2015). In many developed countries, such as Australia, the Government, through the National Vocational Education and Training E-learning strategy, supports the application of mobile technologies in learning thus universities and schools have introduced a mobile learning project for example "Bring Your Own Device" (BYOD), to support students' learning through their own devices (McLean, 2016, p. 2).

The immediate access and flexibility of mobile devices are seen as enablers for collective learning (Falloon, 2015). Sub-Saharan Africa is one of the swiftest growing regions for mobile subscriptions in the world, with a mobile infiltration rate of 75% in 2018 (GSMA, 2018). In 2017, third-generation (3G) connectivity via mobile phone was almost universal in South Africa (GSMA, 2017), while in Kenya, mobile penetration based on SIM connections stood at 91% (Masese & Makena, 2019). Thus, mobile phones are used to support learning in resource-challenged schooling contexts in Africa (Traxler, 2010).

4   Teacher Challenges Concerning the Integration of Mobile Technologies in Their Teaching

Challenges related to teachers' adoption of mobile technologies have emerged from the fact that they are not effectively prepared to investigate the advantages or make informed decisions (Kukulska-Hulme et al., 2009; Schuck et al.,

2013). Other concerns, associated with the integration of new technologies, are the fear of change, motivation, lack of training and expertise, teaching beliefs, self-efficacy, and the school culture (Makoe, 2013; Ertmer & Ottenbreit-Leftwich, 2010). According to Ertmer and Ottenbreit-Leftwich (2010), teachers need a paradigm shift to adjust their traditional pedagogic practices.

An obstacle that prevents teachers in the United Kingdom, from integrating technology in their teaching is finding time for planning and exploring the effectiveness of the plan (Haydn, 2001). Within the South African context (more so in rural communities) most teachers are concerned about an increased workload (Makoe, 2013). The literature discussed above anticipates the challenges in pedagogical practice when mobile technologies are incorporated within classroom teaching. This study draws attention to the intricacy of integrating mobile technologies in teaching, using, Mishra and Koehler's (2006, p. 1029) 'Technological, Pedagogical and Content Knowledge' model.

5 Theoretical Framing

Mishra and Koehler (2006) suggested the use of Technological, Pedagogical and Content Knowledge framework for integrating technology when teaching and learning. The Technological, Pedagogical and Content Knowledge (TPACK) model is an extension of Shulman's (1986, p. 8) model of Pedagogical Content Knowledge (PCK). Shulman critiqued teacher education programmes for the isolation of content knowledge and pedagogical knowledge. Shulman argued that content and pedagogy are intrinsically interrelated; hence, pre-service teachers ought to have a deep understanding of both types of knowledge. Mishra and Koehler (2006) adopted Shulman's view and extended the argument to include technology. They assert that since technology has become an important component of the teaching and learning processes, due to its capacity for improving the learning and teaching processes. Thus, teachers need to understand the relationship between the three types of teacher knowledge, specifically content, pedagogy, and technology, as reflected in Figure 8.1.

Teachers require certain competencies to connect the three types of knowledge: content (subject area knowledge), pedagogy (teaching knowledge), and technology (technology background) namely:
– Pedagogical content knowledge (PCK), focuses on Shulman's (1986) idea revolving around how to teach specifically content-based material.
– Technological content knowledge (TCK), focusses on how to choose technologies that best represent and support particular content-based guidelines.
– Technological pedagogical knowledge (TPK), refers to how to use specific technologies when teaching.

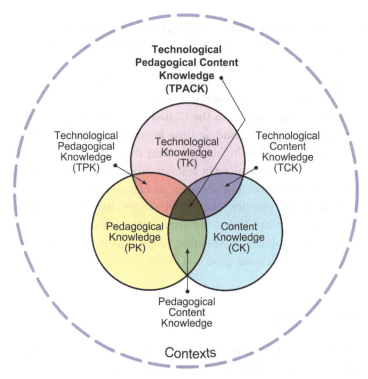

FIGURE 8.1 The TPACK framework (adapted from Koehler, Mishra, Akcaoglu, & Rosenberg, 2013, p. 3; reproduced by permission of the publisher, © 2012 by tpack.org, http://tpack.org)

– Technological pedagogical content knowledge (TPCK/TPACK), refers to how to teach material that is specifically content-based while using technologies that best represent and support it, in ways that are appropriately matched to students' needs and preferences.

The technological knowledge referred to in the TPACK framework is not about computer skills but an elevated awareness of the affordances of emerging technology tools for learning (Bower, 2008). It refers to knowledge about the affordances of emerging technologies that impact teachers' existing priorities and agendas, their concerns, motivations and incentives for use. Studies by Chai, Ling Koh, Tsai, and Lee WeeTan (2011); Harris and Hofer (2011); Koh, Chai, and Tsai (2013); Polly (2011); Hyo-Jeong and Bosung (2009) highlight TPACK's contribution to understanding the complexity of technological and pedagogical practices within schooling contexts. However, it is significant to remember that the TPACK model does not consider the influence of the teachers' socio-cultural background on their use of technologies during teaching. For example, Polly's (2011) study discussed causes for the challenges experienced while enacting TPACK in pedagogical practices, but there is little discussion of teachers' socio-cultural backgrounds when examining participants' TPACK.

Although the TPACK model diagram (Figure 8.1) situates the interconnecting rings/circles in an area marked "context", the model does not specify or define this context. Hence, we argue that TPACK's theorization does not include room for explaining teachers' socio-cultural backgrounds when investigating pedagogical practices.

6 Research Methods and Design

This qualitative interpretative study embraced an ethnographic methodology to explore teacher educators' experiences of using mobile phones in their pedagogical practices. The interpretative paradigm aims to understand the social phenomenon explored from participants' perspectives (Cohen, Manion, & Morrison, 2017). Ethnography seeks to understand a particular group (teacher educators) in their socio-cultural "milieu's" (Charmaz, 2006, p. 40). This means that ethnographic research describes socio-cultural entities in individuals' actions and emphasizes the ground understanding of participants' contexts (Wolcott, 1987). Participant teacher educators in this research worked at a teacher training university in KwaZulu-Natal, Eastwood University (pseudonym), in a specific socio-cultural context, which can influence how they form specific practices. The ethnographic methodology had two foci: institutional (teacher education context) and socio-cultural (the connection between teacher educators' early background and their later formed practices).

Permission to conduct this study was acquired from Eastwood University (pseudonym). Six teacher educators from the mathematics and technology education discipline were purposively selected to participate in this study. These teacher educators teach Intermediate phase, pre-service teachers. The criteria for their selection was they lecture to pre-service teachers who study both mathematics and technology education as their learning areas. The autonomy of the participants was guaranteed using informed consent letters. During phase one of the data generating semi-structured interviews were used to obtain data from six teacher educators. The interviews which were audio-recorded were approximately 45 minutes each. The interview focused on: their home environment, community, schooling, childhood, their use of the cell phone in general, their use of the cell phone during teaching, their experience in using the cell phone to learn/teach mathematics and solve a contextual problem experienced by the community during technology education, perceptions on support available for lecturers to use mobile technologies in their teaching and what enabled or hindered their use of mobile technologies in teaching mathematics and technology education at Eastwood University.

In phase two of data generation, the six teacher educators were observed while lecturing. Observation entails recording the behavioral patterns of participants to gain a deeper insight into the phenomenon being observed (Cohen, Manion, & Morrison, 2017). Observations were used to learn about the teacher educators' lecture room practice relating to the use of mobile technologies in the teaching of mathematics and to document it. Furthermore, the observations were used to validate data from the interview. The following aspects were observed: how the teacher educator used mobile technology in the teaching of mathematics and technology education as well as whether mobile technologies were used in isolation or to contextualize the teaching of mathematics and technology education.

Two lectures were observed per teacher educator, and all observations were video recorded. All audio and video recordings were transcribed verbatim. Transcripts were sent to participants for member checking. According to Creswell and Creswell (2018), member checking enhances the credibility of the study. Member checking allows participants the opportunity to read individual interview transcripts to ensure data was captured correctly on the phenomenon being explored and to avoid misinterpretation by the researcher due to the possibility of mishearing what had been said.

The transcripts were read several times before analysis could begin. During data analysis, coding sketches were used to trace the links between teacher educators' early learning experiences, socio-cultural background and pedagogy and how the mobile phone/s were used in practice.

7   Results and Discussion

In this section, we present the analysis for six teacher educators. Our analysis reveals that four themes emerged.

7.1   *Impact of Early Learning Experience on Pedagogy*

All six teacher educators reflected on the pedagogical techniques that their teachers used as a primary source of their teaching-related knowledge as is implicit in the excerpts below:

> I teach mathematics the way I was taught, chalk and talk method, it's important to master your content, so yes rote learning has its place… (P1, Interview)

> I teach technology education the way I learnt in school, I had an exceptional teacher who always tried new interesting things in class, who challenged us to solve a real problem in our community, so in the same way, I try to challenge my students… (P3, Interview)

Comments made by the teacher educators in the interview seem to concur with the comments made during the observation of lectures.

> The best method to teach math is chalk and talk; it works I am proof of it, you students cannot add three sets of numbers without using a calculator, use your head people, it will help you. I grew up without technology do I am not a slave to it. (P1, Observation)

> Back when I was I school my teacher always made abstract concepts less abstract by using picture or charts, you and I are fortunate to have technology at our disposal to facilitate teaching and learning, use your phones to look at the arch of Moses Maida stadium and establish the types of support used and explain why this is the best support structure. (P3, Observation)

From the preceding excerpts, the contrasting ways in which teacher educators' respective learning experiences influence their pedagogy comes to the fore. Participant 1's appreciation of and the value for rote learning and 'chalk and talk' pedagogy becomes conspicuous. It is evident that P1 valued his teachers' teaching, and, in the process, P1 seems to be oblivious of different teaching strategies, learning theories and different learning styles and favours a teacher-centred approach to teaching. Participant 3 is conscious of the need for innovative pedagogy to promote learning and favours a learner-centred approach that engages the student in inquiry-based learning. The above finding concurs with that of Olesen and Hora's (2014, p. 32) notion that teacher educators do indeed 'teach the way they were taught'. This means that teacher educators' early learning experiences do influence their pedagogy.

7.2 Socio-Cultural Background and Pedagogy

All six teacher educators carry with them their socio-cultural and economic background, assumptions and beliefs into their lecture rooms. In other words, their personalities and pedagogy are sculpted by their socio-cultural interactions. The excerpts that follow, highlight how socio-cultural background impacts teacher educators' pedagogy.

> My culture values education, therefore I actively engage students in different types of activities to encourage them to learn, I believe that teaching is my calling and I enjoy both teaching and research… (P2, Interview)

> My parents emphasized that education is the key to success and a way out of poverty, I am open to learning and use method that helps my students grasp difficult concepts… (P6, Interview)

Teaching was a good option, during apartheid we didn't have many career choices and opportunities available to us, my parents encouraged me to strive for excellence in my career, so I invest a lot of time and energy in my teaching and students, it is a form of Seva,[2] keeping abreast with current teaching pedagogies and using them effectively is important to me… (P4, Interview).

Similar views were expressed during the observation of lectures.

> How you are taught will influence how you will teach, I am exposing you to all the technologies so that you are prepared to teach in the 4IR, you must be innovative to capture your learners' attention. (P5, Observation)

The preceding excerpts reveal how socio-cultural and economic factors impact teacher educators' beliefs, teaching values and ultimately, their pedagogical approaches used in their lecture room. The socio-cultural, economic and historical factors mentioned in the excerpts have shaped these teacher educators' professional identity. Miller (2002) argues that teacher identity is a process of social negotiation, strongly shaped by our socio-cultural experiences and is rooted in historical power.

7.3   *Teacher Educators' Pedagogy*

These teacher educators' pedagogy is an interactive and relational reflective process based on subtle judgments and adaptive responses to their unique students and their learning requirements of what to teach and how to teach as is conspicuous in the excerpts that follow:

> I always need to know what the students already know about a topic, like shapes and their properties, before I introduce them to activities on shapes. This lets me identify any misconceptions or preconceptions they

bring to the class. I adjust my teaching accordingly to show the student how to address the misconceptions during teaching. Most of my students are from previously disadvantaged backgrounds…I come from a similarly disadvantaged background…I understand their struggle. Therefore, it's important to me that they understand and know how to teach math and to make math accessible to learners…using mobile phones to teach math is very beneficial… (P5, Interview)

My students learn from how I act as a teacher as they do from the content I present. When I want them to apply shapes to construct rigid structures, like a temple or bridge, I have to create opportunities for them to engage in such reasoning to develop the necessary skills. If I do not do this, then I will undermine the module outcomes and my own beliefs about training teachers to teach. I always enquire from my students their beliefs about teaching and learning to teach. I let my students know that I gaze at my practice all the time and ask them to let me know how I could improve teaching a particular section… (P3, Interview)

The excerpts from the interview with P3 resonates with the statement from the observation of P3's lecture. The observation that follows demonstrates P3's pedagogy.

I want you to use your phones to observe the Eiffel tower, Great mosque of Djenne and the Parthenon identify what shapes are common and unique to these structures. Work in pairs, you have 5 minutes before you present your answers and then 10 minutes for reflection before we discuss correct and incorrect responses. (P3, Observation)

The preceding excerpts highlight that the teacher educators created the space for their student voices to be heard during their teaching to improve the educational process. They forged a rapport with their students by creating opportunities for active engagement and accessed students' prior learning and preconceptions. The actions of these teacher educators positioned these teacher educators as active learners as they seek input from their students. In their pedagogy, the teacher educators demonstrated awareness of the self as a teacher, awareness of the teaching process, awareness of the student and awareness of context.

According to Lopez and Olan (2018), skilled pedagogy requires a highly developed awareness of the factors at play during teaching. From this understanding of pedagogy, the relational and reflexive nature of teaching becomes apparent. Our finding shows that teacher educators' decisions about their pedagogical strategies are based on their understanding of what it means to teach and how technology would suit their context of practice (Barton & Berchini, 2013). The actions of teacher educators in the above excerpts coincide with what Loughran (2008) regards as pedagogy, knowledge of teaching about teaching and learning about teaching.

7.4 How Teacher Educators used Mobile Phones during Teaching

Teacher educator (P1) does not embrace mobile phones in his pedagogy. The excerpts below bear testimony of his lecture room practice.

> I don't use mobile phones in my teaching…I cannot monitor how students use their phones to learn…I favour chalk and talk…for me students knowing the content is important…it's what would help them in their teaching. I don't use technology in my teaching as I'm afraid my students may know more than me… (P1, Interview)

Excerpts from the observation of his lecture corroborate with the data from the interview.

> Please, you know the rules in my class you are not allowed to have your phones out, it is a distraction to teaching and learning. This is a maths class – you must be able to solve problems on the board and in your books, rote learning is important in math. (P1, Observation)

The above findings reveal the P1 does not embrace the use of mobile technologies in his teaching and finds mobile technologies to be disruptive to teaching and learning. The above findings resonate with that of Dyson, Andrews, Smyth, and Wallace (2013) who found that ringtones in the classroom and texting may significantly disturb pedagogical activities as planned by the teacher. Also, games, music, videos, photos and access to the internet may compromise student performance in class (Dyson et al., 2013). Participant 1's strong earlier learning experience (learning by rote and 'chalk and talk') is dominant in his practice as a teacher educator and influences his TPACK.

Participant 1 strengthened the validity of this finding, as he repeatedly discussed the values of this rote learning. The various ways in which participant teacher educators embrace mobile phones in their pedagogy is conspicuous in the excerpts that follow.

> I fully embrace using mobile technologies in my teaching, it's important to demonstrate to students how to use mobile technologies to facilitate

the learning of content and to make learning real and interesting, also to prepare them to be able to teach in the 4IR... (P2, Interview)

Cell phones help in teaching student's shapes, angles and design...I get students to take photos, videos of geometric shapes in their community or all around them. In class, they then share this in small groups, and each group get a chance to present their discussion to the whole class... (P3, Interview)

I am an avid user of various technologies; students learn and understand concepts better when they use cell phones as a learning device. I get my students to notice math concepts/ content outside the lecture room. They don't see maths as occurring in their local environment and think it's too abstract confined to textbook and classrooms only. Through the use of cell phones, I have placed mathematical concepts in real-life situations, thereby contextualizing learning and making math concepts more accessible to the student. I find inspiration in my surrounding to design activities where students have to apply their knowledge of shapes and angles to create rigid structures I'm ok with learning from my students about the various apps that can be used in teaching maths and technology education... (P6, Interview)

Comments made by the teacher educators in the interview seem to concur with the comments made during the observation of lectures.

The pictures you captured yesterday with your mobile phone are excellent examples of math shapes used in structures. I want you to focus on your photos and search for fractions within them example halves, quarters etc. after that convert the fractions observed into decimals. In this activity, you will be able to see math occurring in everyday contexts. (P2, Observation)

Your task is to investigate the different angles and shapes in your home and place of worship. (P4, Observation)

I want you to use your phones, to take pictures of various equipment and structures in the university Gymnasium, study these pictures and write down what mechanisms are used to reinforce or support these structure. (P6, Observation)

The preceding excerpts reveal the use of mobile smartphones to make students more aware of mathematics in everyday life and to initiate their thinking about mathematics within real-life contexts. This action of teacher educators (except for P1) enables students to move from the concrete (observing phenomena) to the abstract (understanding the principles or theories that are derived from the observation of phenomena and then apply it to design and solve contextualized problems. In the process, enhancing students' recognition and observation skills, discussion and presentation skills and developing more positive attitudes towards mathematics was exhibited. The use of mobile phones has advanced these teacher educators' pedagogy as they see their surroundings as a source of inspiration to design mathematics and technology education lectures. These findings are aligned with those of Tangney, Weber, O'Hanlon, Knowles, Munnelly, Salkham, and Jennings' (2010) findings, which indicated that smartphones could be used to support collaborative and contextualized learning as well as extend mathematical thinking and enhance problem-solving procedures.

Participant 2's cultural values influence her belief about education and her pedagogy. Participant 2 embraces a student-centred approach to her teaching and engages her students with various interactive strategies. Her TPACK allowed her to use technologies to make her teaching interactive, efficient, and creative and to demonstrate to students the value of using technologies to facilitate and contextualize learning.

The innovative teaching P3 encountered as a child has sculpted her teaching identity and influenced her beliefs about the role of teachers and her pedagogy. Participant 3 is a reflexive practitioner who uses her students as a mirror to gaze inward. Her TPACK is shaped by her pedagogical philosophy, which is grounded by socio-cultural factors that P3 experienced as a learner.

Participant 4's strong cultural belief has influenced his teacher identity and pedagogical practice and TPACK. Participant 5's earlier socio-economic background has influenced his outlook towards his students and his pedagogy and TPACK. Her interest affects P6's TPACK in technology. Participant 6 uses the mobile phone to contextualize mathematics for her students effectively. Socio-cultural factors influence her TPACK and pedagogy.

8   Conclusion

Our findings show that teacher educators' pedagogical and technological practices are influenced by their identities, early learning experiences and socio-cultural background. Researchers (Cheng, Cheng, & Tang, 2010; Gay, 2010; Wong, 2005) draw attention to the importance of understanding individuals' socio-cultural background when explaining their pedagogical practices. It is worth mentioning that even though the teacher educators in this study came from diverse socio-cultural backgrounds, their socio-cultural background and the context where they teach influenced their pedagogical and technological practices.

Thus, this study proposes that the TPACK framework needs to include a socio-cultural dimension to understand teacher educators' existing pedagogical practices with technology concerning their socio-cultural background. The extended TPACK framework is relevant to explain the connection between technology, pedagogy and socio-cultural background.

The extended TPACK framework is useful for analyzing teachers' past and present experiences when investigating their pedagogical and technological practice. It would help to identify which aspects need to be considered when designing teachers' professional development.

Notes

1 Participants were coded as Participant 1 (P1), participant 2 (P2) and so on.
2 Seva means selfless service in Sanskrit.

References

Barton, A. C., & Berchini, C. (2013). Becoming an insider: Teaching science in urban settings. *Theory into Practice, 52*(1), 21–27. doi:10.1080/07351690.2013.743765

Bower, M. (2008). Affordance analysis-matching learning tasks with learning technologies. *Educational Media International, 45*(1), 3–15.

Chai, C. S., Ling Koh, J. H., Tsai, C. C., & Lee Wee Tan, L. (2011). Modeling primary school pre-service teachers' Technological Pedagogical Content Knowledge (TPACK) for meaningful learning with Information and Communication Technology (ICT). *Computers and Education, 57*(1), 1184–1193.

Charmaz, K. (2016). *Constructing grounded theory: A practical guide through qualitative analysis.* Sage Publications.

Cheng, M. M. H., Cheng, A. Y. N., & Tang, S. Y. F. (2010). Closing the gap between the theory and practice of teaching: Implications for teacher education programmes in Hong Kong. *Journal of Education for Teaching, 36*(1), 91–104. doi:10.1080/02607470903462222

Cheon, J., Lee, S., Crooks, S. M., & Song, J. (2012). An investigation of mobile learning readiness in higher education based on the theory of planned behaviour. *Computers and Education, 59*(3), 1054–1064.

Cohen, L., Manion, L., & Morrison, K. (2017). *Research methods in education.* Routledge Taylor and Francis Group.

Creswell, J. W., & Creswell, J. D. (2018). *Research design: Qualitative, quantitative, and mixed methods approaches.* Sage Publications.

Dyson, L. E., Andrews, T., Smyth, R., & Wallace, R. (2013). Towards a holistic framework for ethical mobile learning. In Z. Berg & L. Muilenberg (Eds.), *The Routledge handbook of mobile learning* (pp. 405–416). Routledge.

Ekanayake, S. Y., & Wishart, J. (2014). Integrating mobile phones into teaching and learning: A case study of teacher training through professional development workshops. *British Journal of Educational Technology, 46*(2), 173–189. doi:10.1111/bjet.12131

Ertmer, P. A., & Ottenbreit-Leftwich, A. T. (2010). Teacher technology change: How knowledge, confidence, belief, and culture intersect. *Journal of Research on Technology in Education, 42*(3), 255–284.

Falloon, G. (2015). What's the difference? Learning collaboratively using iPads in conventional classrooms. *Computers and Education, 84*(1), 62–77. doi:10.1016/j.compedu.2015.01.010

Frohberg, D. D., Göth, C. C., & Schwabe, G. G. (2009). Mobile learning projects-A critical analysis of the state of the art. *Journal of Computer Assisted Learning, 25*(4), 307–331.

Gay, G. (2010). *Culturally responsive teaching: Theory, research, and practice* (2nd ed.). New York Teachers College.

GSMA. (2017). *The mobile economy Sub-Saharan Africa 2017.* Author. Retrieved November 10, 2019, from https://www.gsmaintelligence.com/research/?file=7bf3592e6d750144e58d9dcfac6adfab&download

GSMA. (2018). *The mobile economy 2018.* Author. Retrieved November 10, 2019, from https://www.gsma.com/mobileeconomy/wp-content/uploads/2018/05/The-Mobile-Economy-2018.pdf

Harris, J. B., & Hofer, M. J. (2011). Technological Pedagogical Content Knowledge (TPACK) in action: A descriptive study of secondary teachers' curriculum-based, technology-related instructional planning. *Journal of Research on Technology in Education, 43*(3), 211–229.

Haydn, T. (2001). Subject discipline dimensions of ICT and learning: History; A case study. *International Journal of Historical Learning, Teaching and Research, 2*(1), 1–19.

Hyo-Jeong, S., & Bosung, K. (2009). Learning about problem-based learning: Student teachers integrating technology, pedagogy and content knowledge. *Australasian Journal of Educational Technology, 25*(1), 101–116.

Jalil, A., Beer, M., & Crowther, P. (2015). Pedagogical requirements for mobile learning: A review on MOBIlearn task Model. *Journal of Interactive Media in Education, 12*(1), 1–17. http://dx.doi.org/10.5334/jime.ap

Jita, T. (2018). Exploring pre-service teachers' opportunities to learn to teach science with ICTs during teaching practice. *Journal of Education, 71*(1), 74–90. http://dx.doi.org/10.17159/2520-9868/i71a05

Kearney, M., & Maher, D. (2013). Mobile learning in mathematics teacher education: Using iPads to support pre-service teachers' professional development. *Australian Educational Computing, 27*(3), 76–84.

Kearney, M., Schuck, S., Burden, K., & Aubusson, P. (2012). Viewing mobile learning from a pedagogical perspective. *Research in Learning Technology, 20*(1), 1–17. http://dx.doi.org/10.3402/rlt.v20i0.14406

Kenny, R. F., Park, C. L, Van Neste-Kenny, J. M. C., Burton, P. A., & Meiers, J. (2009). M-learning in nursing practice education: Applying Koole's FRAME model. *Journal of Distance Education, 23*(3), 75–96.

Koehler, M. J., Mishra, P., Akcaoglu, M., & Rosenberg, J. M. (2013). *The technological pedagogical content knowledge framework for teachers and teacher educators ICT integrated teacher education models* (pp. 1–6). CEMCA.

Koh, J. H. L., Chai, C. S., & Tsai, C. C. (2013). Examining practicing teachers' perceptions of Technological Pedagogical Content Knowledge (TPACK) pathways: A structural equation modeling approach. *Instructional Science, 41*(4), 793–809.

Kukulska-Hulme, A., Sharples, M., Milrad, M., Arnedillo-Sánchez, I., & Vavoula, G. (2009). Innovation in mobile learning: A European perspective. *International Journal of Mobile and Blended Learning, 1*(1), 13–35.

Kynäslahti, H. (2003). In search of elements of mobility in the context of education. In H. Kynäslahti & P. Seppälä (Eds.), *Mobile learning* (pp. 41–48). IT Press.

Lopez, A. E., & Olan, E. L. (Eds.). (2018). *Transformative pedagogies for teacher education: Moving towards praxis in an era of change* (pp. 123–140). Information Age Publishing, Inc.

Loughran, J. J. (2008). Toward a better understanding of teaching and learning about teaching. In M. Cochran-Smith, S. Feiman-Nemser, D. J. McIntyre, & K. E. Demers (Eds.), *Handbook of research on teacher education* (3rd ed., pp. 1177–1182). Routledge.

Makoe, M. (2013). Teachers as learners. Concerns and perceptions about using cell phones in South African rural communities. In Z. L. Berge & L. Y. Muilenburg (Eds.), *Handbook of mobile learning*. Routledge.

Masese, P., & Makena, L. (2019). *Kenya mobile report 2019*. Retrieved July 25, 2019, from https://www.jumia.co.ke/mobile-report/

McLean, K. (2016). The Implementation of Bring Your Own Device (BYOD) in primary [elementary] schools. *Frontiers in Psychology, 7*, 1–3. doi:10.3389/fpsyg.2016.01739

Miller, M. M. (2002). Examining the discourses that shape our teacher identities. *Curriculum Inquiry, 32*(1), 453–469.

Mishra, P., & Koehler, M. J. (2006). Technological pedagogical content knowledge: A framework for integrating technology in teachers' knowledge. *Teachers College Record, 108*(6), 1017–1054.

Ngesi, N., Landa, N., Madikiza, N., Cekiso, M. P., Tshotsho, B., & Walters, L. M. (2018). Use of mobile phones as supplementary teaching and learning tools to learners in South Africa. *Reading & Writing, 9*(1), a190. https://doi.org/10.4102/rw.v9i1.190

North, D., Johnston, K., & Ophoff, J. (2014). The use of mobile phones by South African university student. *Issues in Informing Science and Information Technology, 11*(1), 115–138. http://iisit.org/Vol11/IISITv11p115-138

Olesen, A., & Hora, M. T. (2014). Teaching the way they were taught? Revisiting the sources of teaching knowledge and the role of prior experience in shaping faculty teaching practices. *Higher Education, 68*(1), 29–45.

Ozdamli, F., & Cavus, N. (2011). Basic elements and characteristics of mobile learning. *Procedia-Social and Behavioral Sciences, 28*(1), 937–942.

Parsons, D., & Ryu, H. (2006). A framework for assessing the quality of mobile learning. In R. Dawson, E. Georgiadou, P. Lincar, M. Ross, & G. Staples (Eds.), *Learning and teaching issues in software quality, Proceedings of the 11th international conference for process improvement, research and education* (pp. 17–27).

Polly, D. (2011). Examining teachers' enactment of Technological Pedagogical and Content Knowledge (TPACK) in their mathematics teaching after technology integration professional development. *Journal of Computers, Mathematics and Science Teaching, 30*(1), 37–59.

Schuck, S., Aubusson, P., Kearney, M., & Burden, K. (2013). Mobilizing teacher education: A study of a professional learning community. *Teacher Development, 17*(1), 1–18.

Sharples, M., Arnedillo-Sánchez, I., Milrad, M., & Vavoula, G. (2009). Mobile learning: Small devices, big issues. In S. Ludvigsen, N. Balacheff, T. D. Jong, A. Lazonder, & S. Barnes (Eds.), *Technology-enhanced learning: Principles and products* (pp. 233–249). Springer-Verlag.

Shulman, L. S. (1986). Those who understand: Knowledge growth in teaching. *Educational Researcher, 15*(2), 4–14.

Tangney, B., Weber, S., O'Hanlon, P., Knowles, D., Munnelly, J., Salkham, A., & Jennings, K. (2010). 'Mobi Maths': An approach to utilizing smartphones in teaching mathematics. In M. Montebello, V. Camilleri, & A. Dingli (Eds.), *Proceedings of mLearn2010: 10th world conference on mobile and contextual learning* (pp. 9–15). University of Malta, Valetta.

Traxler, J. (2010). Students and mobile devices. *ALT-J, Research in Learning Technology, 18*(2), 149–160. https://doi.org/10.1080/09687769.2010.492847

Valk, J.-H., Rashid, A. T., & Elder, L. (2010). Using mobile phones to improve educational outcomes: An analysis of evidence from Asia. *International Review of Research in Open and Distance Learning, 11*(1), 117–140.

Wolcott, H. F. (1987). On ethnographic intent. In G. Spindler & L. Spindler (Eds.), *Interpretive ethnography of education* (pp. 37–57). Lawrence Erlbaum.

Wong, M. (2005). A cross-cultural comparison of teachers' expressed beliefs about music education and their observed practices in classroom music teaching. *Teachers and Teaching, 11*(4), 397–418. doi:10.1080/13450600500137182

PART 4

The 21st-Century Student

CHAPTER 9

Teaching and Learning Science in the 21st Century: A Study of Critical Thinking of Learners and Associated Challenges

Yashwantrao Ramma, Ajeevsing Bholoa, Shobha Jawaheer, Sandhya Gunness, Henri Tin Yan Li Kam Wah, Ajit Kumar Gopee and Deewarkarsingh Authelsingh

Abstract

The teaching and learning of science entail a set of complex and interrelated tasks and skills ranging from testing prior knowledge to eventually connecting newly constructed knowledge to real-life situations. Yet, there is still little research reporting how teachers make instructional decisions based on learners' prior knowledge in this technological-driven era, characterizing the Fourth Industrial Revolution. One of the aims of teaching and learning science is to promote learners' scientific reasoning and critical thinking through a process of criticality. Available studies show that teachers still encounter difficulties tapping on learners' prior knowledge through the use of appropriate instructional practices during their lessons to foster critical thinking. A study was conducted to investigate the extent to which science students had developed a critical mind through scientific reasoning at the secondary school level, and to reflect on the subsequent implications at tertiary level in Mauritius. Questionnaires on an issue related to a power cut problem and with a focus on three levels of critical thinking, i.e. thinking, reflecting, and action was administered to a representative sample of students. Selected participants were then interviewed to corroborate findings from the initial data set. One of the key findings of this study is that science students at secondary and tertiary levels have developed limited critical thinking, based on their prior knowledge, to correctly assess a given contextual situation and eventually make the appropriate decision. The findings stemming from this study have far-reaching implications for the teaching and learning of science in the Mauritian and global education systems.

1   Introduction

Although a rapid development in digital educational technology should facilitate the teaching and learning of science, the latter is becoming more and more challenging. Osborne (2014, p. 54) contends that "science is often taught more as dogma a set of unequivocal, uncontested and unquestioned facts more akin to the way people are indoctrinated into faith than into a critical, questioning community". Such a practice is, unfortunately, still predominant in this technological era in many education systems (Isseks, 2011; Timothy, Feldhaus, & Bentrem, 2013). Students have to be equipped with the necessary scientific skills for citizenship, work, life and preparedness for the demands of the Fourth Industrial Revolution (4IR) so that they can address societal challenges (Scott, 2015). The World Economic Forum in its publication, New Vision for Education: Unlocking the Potential of Technology (WEF, 2015), lists three major areas, namely, foundational literacies, competencies and character qualities as being the foundation for the 21st-century skills. Sixteen skills, among which critical thinking/problem-solving, creativity, curiosity, and Information Communication Technology (ICT) literacy without downplaying the soft skills (such as leadership, collaboration, and social and cultural awareness) are encompassed within these three major areas. Critical thinking, problem-solving, creativity and curiosity have always been at the forefront of the process for scientific investigations and experimentation, which lie at the heart of the construction of scientific knowledge by learners. To optimize students' scientific competencies, systematic and high-level classroom processes, curriculum and learning time, the instructional quality of science teaching and learning and a supportive classroom climate need to be reviewed (Müller, Prenzel, Seidel, Schiepe-Tiska, & Kjærnsli, 2016).

Learning science is important for everyone according to the National Academies Press, (NAP, 2012), even for those who would later not choose careers in the fields of Science, Technology, Engineering and Mathematics (STEM). In fact, in this "post-scientific society" (Hill, 2008), due to the growing human impact on the world, a scientifically literate society is essential for the decision-making process (SAPEA, 2019; Glaze, 2018) in every task that someone has to undertake. Concerning STEM-related subjects, learners are required to engage in critical thinking, which requires "reasonable reflective thinking focused on deciding what to believe or do" (Ennis, 2015, p. 32).

Thus, teachers have the opportunity during group work to engage learners in critical thinking, through several structured activities (Burke, 2011), to enable them to assimilate the new knowledge into their pre-existing framework. However, though prior knowledge is the building block for further learning, it can nevertheless be a barrier to learning (National Research Council, 2005). It is argued that with experience and judicious use of prior knowledge, coupled with the teacher's support, learners will develop a critical mind. This involves undertaking structured thinking in a context-specific situation (Byrne & Brodie, 2012; Fields, 2019). By asking the right question to assess, in the first instance, the occurrence of a situation and then attempt to address it by tapping on fundamental skills (Gyenes, 2015) such as creative thinking, autonomy, problem evaluation, analysis and interpretation, real-life reasoning and problem-solving. During that process, it is generally thought that it is important to promote a critical mind in science education (Bailin, 2002). However, just learning about developing a critical mind does not lead to the development of a critical attitude towards social issues unless it is tied to argumentation and decision-making through a process of "criticality" (Davies, 2015, p. 65). This entails thinking, reflecting and acting (Barnett, 1997).

Furthermore, learning is not a simple endeavor; it involves "mastering abstract principles, understanding proofs, remembering factual information, acquiring methods, techniques and approaches, recognition, reasoning, debating ideas, or developing behavior appropriate to specific situations" (Fry, Ketteridge, & Marshall, 2009, p. 8). Today's society is increasingly technologically, and information-driven and the ability to think critically at an early age has become a keystone to face and compete in everyday life (Stein, Haynes, Redding, Ennis, & Cecil, 2007; Cuban, 2001). However, in practice, STEM educators tend to adopt traditional teaching approaches (Ramma, Samy, & Gopee, 2015) such as content-based teaching. This, as described by Osborne (2014), involves teaching science as a set of unequivocal, uncontested and unquestioned facts. It also involves resorting to students' memorization skills for their learning rather than promoting critical thinking. The view adopted by the National Research Council, namely, that "Learning science is something students do, not something that is done to them" (National Research Council, 1996, p. 20) rightly presents science as a process of knowledge construction and acquisition. This standpoint is further supported by Osborne (2014, p. 53) who argues that "[c]ritique and questioning are central to the practice of science; without argument and evaluation, the construction of reliable knowledge would be impossible". Teaching and learning science through inquiry in educational institutions has the potential to develop an inquisitive mind in students by allowing them to explore a given phenomenon and walk through several processes while reflecting on their journey (Hofstein & Lunetta, 2003; Fitzgerald, Danaia, & McKinnon, 2019). Such an inquiry approach to teaching and learning is no doubt a challenging task for both teachers and students, especially in the traditional classroom set-up when even universities are failing to equip their students with critical thinking skills (Flores, Matkin, Burbach, Quinn, & Harding, 2012). Ultimately, the students are not in a position to consistently apply their limited pre-existing knowledge to a new situation (Giselsson, 2020). The formulation of an in-built strategy for adopting inquiry by teachers rests extensively on ongoing teachers' professional development (Blank, de las Alas, & Smith, 2008; Tondeur, et al., 2012; Fitzgerald, Danaia, & McKinnon, 2019).

Many factors, like limited professional development, insufficient time, limited collaboration, out-of-hours preparatory work (Fitzgerald, Danaia, & McKinnon, 2019) have been attributed to the difficulty that both teachers and students encounter in the adoption of inquiry as a classroom strategy for knowledge construction by the latter. Furthermore, the difficulty becomes even more prominent when ICT is embedded in science lessons alongside the traditional approach (Devlin, Feldhaus, & Bentrem, 2013). Sointu, Hirsto, and Murtonen (2019, p. 1) uphold the view that student-centered learning in the 21st century demands a novel consideration for teaching and learning, which "necessitates the development of pedagogical thinking, technical infrastructure, and learning environments". The learning environment within shared social contexts is a pre-requisite for learners to develop a shared understanding of concepts (Hume & Coll, 2010) as, for one to "think critically, one needs to have something to think about" (Lloyd & Bahr, 2010).

The study is aimed at investigating the critical thinking ability of students when confronted with a real-life problem, namely a power cut problem. To define the scope and purpose of the study, the following research questions were formulated:

1. To what extent do students at secondary (age range 16–18 years) and tertiary levels (age range 19–21 years) demonstrate critical thinking while analysing a power cut problem at their home place?
2. How do the students relate their prior knowledge of science to the power cut problem?

The research hypotheses were:
– Students (secondary and tertiary levels) perform equally well in the three levels of criticality (thinking, reflecting and action);
– Tertiary level students have a higher critical thinking ability than secondary level students.

2 Methodology

Both quantitative and qualitative methods were used to generate data that explored how students used their prior knowledge in their critical thinking to deal with a given power cut situation at their home place.

Data from the two methods were used, through triangulation, to identify convergence, corroboration and correspondence of the findings (Caracelli & Green, 1993) and to extend the range of the inquiry. The qualitative data were used to refine the findings from the quantitative data (Creswell, 2012) during the triangulation process. The mixed-method research design was adopted to offset the weaknesses of either method used alone (Rossman & Wilson, 1994). For instance, the semi-structured interviews provided rich details on issues related to the students' thinking that could not have been obtained from the questionnaires alone. As such, the data from the semi-structured interviews helped to clarify and interpret data from the questionnaires. In addition to providing a system of checks and balances, thereby enhancing the validity of the results (Waysman & Savaya, 1997). It should be emphasized that concurrent mixed analyses (Combs & Onwuegbuzie, 2010) were conducted in such a way that the analytical strands do not necessarily occur in chronological order (Teddlie, Tashakkori, & Johnson, 2008).

2.1 *Participants*

The sample constitutes State Secondary Schools students in the A-level secondary level science stream [S(A)] and first-year science stream students in one of the Tertiary Education Institutions (TEIs), as illustrated in Table 9.1.

TABLE 9.1 Frequency distribution

Sample	A-level	TEI
Participants [Questionnaires]	78	150
Participants [Group interviews]	4	3

Necessary ethical clearance was sought from the institutions concerned before implementing the study. Besides, consent was sought from all participants. A consent form was signed by those who had agreed to be group interviewed for 45–50 minutes. For A-level students, a consent form that had to be signed by their parents was issued. The questionnaires were administered via Google Form to all students through the Rectors of all the State Secondary Schools. The selection of the four A-level and TEI participants was based on their responses in the questionnaires. The responses principally encapsulated the three levels of critical thinking, as described in the subsequent sections. The interviews took place at the first author's institution [TEI 03 Nov 2017; S(A) 22 Nov 2017] on two separate occasions and were video recorded with the consent of the interviewees (and of parents for the S(A)).

3 Theoretical Framing

To guide the researchers' understanding and analysis of the respondents' responses related to a particular real-life situation a power cut problem, a framework constituting three levels of critical thinking (Barnett, 1997) was developed then pilot tested. The pilot test was conducted with three students not forming part of the sample. The initial scenario (Figure 9.1) was adopted without modification. The scenario was intentionally developed with a broad perspective where decisions are not expected to be clear-cut (Fortus, Krajcik, Dershimer, Marx, & Mamlok-Naaman, 2005). This would enable the researchers to situate the extent to which the respondents were able to connect content and context (Ramma, Bholoa, Watts, & Nadal, 2018) and to plug in the scientific knowledge acquired in their science lessons to deal with a situation that occurred in their immediate home environment.

Consider the following scenario:

You are watching TV at night at your homeplace and suddenly the power in the room goes out. List all the stages which pertain to your thinking at that instant, in chronological order.

FIGURE 9.1   Power cut problem

The three levels of critical thinking: thinking, reflecting and action (Barnett, 1997) and the description of these levels used to analyse the participants' responses to the power cut problem are illustrated in Table 9.2.

4 Findings and Analysis

Data from each questionnaire referred to as questionnaire one and questionnaire two were administered to the A-level and first-year TEI students respectively and systematically analysed while considering the flow of ideas captured (Table 9.3) in juxtaposition with the description items highlighted in Table 9.2. Each statement of the participants was rated a score of 0, 0.5 or 1, reflecting absence of, partial or adequately structured elements of critical thinking respectively in each of the three levels of criticality as illustrated in Table 9.3. Furthermore, in the same table, a brief insight into the data captured from both sets of questionnaires and the respective marks assigned for statistical analysis are given.

TABLE 9.2 Process of criticality

Process of criticality	Critical thinking stage	Description [regarding the current situation]
Thinking	Elementary [What happened?]	*Is it a general power cut in my room/house or my locality?* *What tool do I need to operate during the power cut?*
Reflecting	Elementary [What course of action do I follow?]	*How do I confirm that it is in the room/house/locality?*
	Intermediate [How do I confirm my hypotheses? What do I conclude? Do I ask for help?]	*How do I verify whether it is a general power cut, or it is in this room/house only?* *What could be the causes of this power cut?*
Action	Advanced [If the issue is local, how do I proceed to solve it? If it is not local, what alternatives do I have?]	*How do I proceed to clarify the questions raised?* *What course of action do I take during the power cut period?* *What technological tools do I have access to help me in my course of action?*

The performance (average scores) of the participants is shown in Table 9.4 and illustrated graphically in Figure 9.2.

In the 'thinking' category, the secondary school students ($N = 78$) averaged a score of 0.65. This score was greater than the average score of 0.45 obtained by TEI students ($N = 150$). Both categories of students fared less well in the subsequent areas of critical thinking, as shown by the lower average scores for 'reflecting' and 'action'. While the secondary school students had a higher average score than the tertiary level students in 'reflecting', the opposite situation prevailed in the 'action' category.

We report two sets of Friedman's tests that were conducted to test at 5% level of significance ($\alpha = 0.05$) the null hypothesis (H_0) whether the distributions for (i) secondary school students and (ii) tertiary students were the same across the three levels of criticality. We used Friedman's test because there is

TABLE 9.3 Overview of findings from questionnaires 1 & 2

Process of criticality	Insights into data from questionnaires 1 (A-level) & 2 (TEI)
Thinking *Elementary*	*Unplug the Mains supply of the TV.* [1, 0, 0 mark] *I would panic because I'm scared of darkness, then I would try to find some light to comfort myself.* [0.5, 0, 0] *Find a candle.* [0.5, 0, 0] *When will power be established?* [0, 0, 0 mark] *Search for a torch.* [1, 0, 0] *Use my mobile phone as a source of light.* [0.5, 0, 0]
Reflecting *Elementary & Intermediate*	*Use a torch to check for the electrical connection issues. If there is no problem, go to bed.* [1, 1, 0] *Search for a candle, light it up, go and check the main switch.* [1, 1, 0] *To check the breaker. To tell parents. To be cautious.* [1, 1, 0] *Is it a general power cut, or is it the circuit breaker? Go and see if the circuit breaker is ok. Wait for the power to come back if it is a general power cut.* [1, 1, 0] *Check if power has gone out in other rooms. Check if neighbours face the same problem. Look for candles. Check mains power supply.* [1, 1, 0] *Should try and see if the light will turn on. If yes, then the problem is with the TV. If not, then it's a power cut. I will wait for the power to come, a maximum of 15 minutes. If it doesn't, I will go to sleep.* [1, 1, 0] *Get phone and turn on the "torch" mode. Look outside to know if neighbours too have this power cut. Wait till power is back on or ask someone to check the breaker.* [1, 1, 0]
Action *Advanced*	*Close the switch to which the TV is connected. Look outside if the streetlights are on. If on, I'll go to check my mains supply. If the Mains is ok, I will call the electricity provider in the morning for maintenance.* [1, 1, 1] *Turn on the mobile flashlight. See if other rooms are also off. If lights outside are on, then check the room breaker or else check the mains breaker and call for help.* [1, 1, 1] *See if the whole house is affected. Switch off power on TV socket. Check if there is power at neighbours' place and on a public light post. If yes, go and check the breaker. If no, turn off all switches and close all windows and go to sleep.* [1, 1, 1]

TABLE 9.4   Average scores of participants in the power cut problem

Category	Thinking	Reflecting	Action
A-level students: S(A)	0.65	0.31	0.13
TEI students	0.48	0.21	0.21

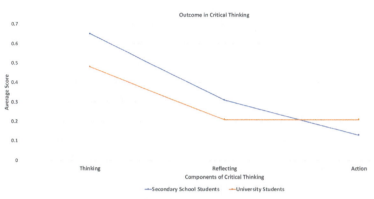

FIGURE 9.2   Outcome in critical thinking

one independent variable (score/mark from the power cut problem) and three levels of criticality (thinking, reflecting and action) and the design is correlated-groups (Jackson, 2010). Furthermore, the Wilcoxon Signed Rank Test was subsequently employed for the post-hoc analysis of significant results.

We conducted Mann-Whitney U tests (Nachar, 2008) to determine (at α = 0.05) whether there were differences in the (median) scores in the areas of 'thinking', 'reflecting' and 'action' between the unrelated and independent groups of secondary school and tertiary level students. To compensate for the Type 1 error inflation as a result of the multiple sample contrasts, we adjusted the level of risk (αB) using Bonferroni's procedure (Corder & Foreman, 2009). In our case, we were making 3 comparisons, so that $\alpha B = 0.05/3 = 0.017$.

The χ^2 statistic from Friedman's test of A-level students is 44.2756 (df = 2, N = 78, $p\text{-value} < 0.00001$). The result was significant at 5%.

The post-hoc analyses for the secondary school students demonstrated significant results in each of the three comparisons, and the data indicated that the performance of the students declined as they progressed from 'thinking', to 'reflecting' and taking 'action'.

The χ^2 statistic from Friedman's test of TEI students is 54.50 (df = 2, N = 150, $p\text{-value} < 0.00001$). The result was significant at 5%.

TABLE 9.5   Post-hoc analysis (Wilcoxon signed-rank test) for secondary school students

Treatments	Statistics	Results at α_B = 0.017
Thinking – reflecting	$W = 0$ ($N = 40$) $z = -5.5109$ (p-value < 0.00001)	Significant
Thinking – action	$W = 14$ ($N = 55$) $z = -6.3342$ (p-value < 0.00001)	Significant
Reflecting – action	$W = 8.5$ ($W_{critical} = 29$, $N = 16$) $z = -3.0767$ (p-value = 0.00208)	Significant

TABLE 9.6   Post-hoc analysis (Wilcoxon signed-rank test) for tertiary students

Treatments	Statistics	Results at α = 0.05
Thinking – reflecting	$W = 27$ ($N = 67$) $z = -6.9463$ (p-value < 0.00001)	Significant
Thinking – action	$W = 27$ ($N = 82$) $z = -7.7411$ (p-value < 0.00001)	Significant
Reflecting – action	$W = 0$ ($W_{critical} = 25$, $N = 15$) $z = -3.4078$ (p-value = 0.00064)	Significant

TABLE 9.7   Mann-Whitney U tests

Treatments	Statistics	Results at α = 0.05	Effect size
Thinking	$U = 4499$ $z = -2.85808$ (p-value = 0.00424)	Significant	0.189
Reflecting	$U = 5298$ $z = -1.16715$ (p-value = 0.242)	Not significant	0.077
Action	$U = 6763$ $z = -0.18306$ (p-value = 0.85716)	Not significant	0.012

The outcomes of the tests related to the tertiary level students were similar to the ones obtained for the secondary school students. It could be noted that there was a gradual decline in the performance of the students across the three areas of critical thinking.

We ran the Mann-Whitney U tests to evaluate the difference in the responses of secondary school and tertiary level students concerning 'thinking', 'reflecting' and 'action'.

The test was significant ($\alpha = 0.05$) for the 'thinking' level while the results for the areas of 'reflecting' and 'action' were non-significant. Therefore, at 5% level of significance, it was likely that the observed differences in the scores of secondary school and tertiary level students were due to random chance. Also, the size effect was relatively small, thereby indicating that, in each case, there was a weak association between the two variables.

The students, both from A-Level [S(A)] and Tertiary Education Institutions (TEIS), displayed a surprisingly low score for items 'reflection' and 'action' concerning our initial hypothesis. However, the A-level students scored better in the 'thinking' and 'reflecting' levels and the answers they offered in the questionnaires were more focused on the context directly related to their immediate environment. For example: *"...look for a source of light" as they were "scared of darkness...and would try to find some light to comfort me...".* On the other hand, the TEI students were more focused on the 'action'. They had regrettably missed the preliminary and intermediate critical thinking levels in the analysis of the power cut issue. Though the difference was relatively small, we had expected the TEI students to score better than the secondary school students while being engaged in the process of criticality, but this had not been the case. The interviews for both categories of students brought further insights into this paradoxical situation. In secondary schools, the teaching and learning of science are traditional (Ramma, Samy, & Gopee, 2015) and most of the teaching time is predominately devoted to the dictation of notes.

The students explained that:

> S(A)1: ...we are so used to getting notes from the teacher without much explanation being offered...
> S(A)2: ...we like getting notes because it is easier for us to pass the exams. During private tuition also we do get notes...

The students confirmed that the drill and practice model was preferred by both the teacher and students and, at times, technology paved its way in the traditional classroom set-up as emphasized by Devlin, Feldhaus, & Bentrem (2013).

> S(A)3: ...sometimes the science teacher makes a PowerPoint presentation or just presents a video on the topic...

They also raised an important point, namely that group work was carried out in subjects other than science. However, group work was not the sole determining criterion to help students develop critical thinking unless the teachers facilitated the process for conducive collaborative learning (Burke, 2011). We learnt from the interview that group work, although occasionally set-up, provided students with the opportunity to think aloud about some phenomena (National Research Council, 2005) and to share their ideas in a formal set-up.

> S(A)3: ...in some classes, we had group work in the subjects like General Paper, French but not in science. Maybe they [the teachers] should have taught us how to do our work on our own, like which website to refer to or they should have told us to go to the library to do independent work...

Furthermore, S(A)2 explained that she was lucky to have engaged in self-learning as she had participated in competitions for secondary schools and her involvement had made her adopt a somewhat different way of thinking. She further added that she now understood the importance of co-curricular activities for the development of self-efficacy (Giselsson, 2020) and independent learning.

> S(A)2: ...my first experience of thinking by myself has been during my participation in the United Nations competition. You have to research all the things by yourself, and this is when I realized how much time it takes to know a subject properly...I have to acknowledge that the teacher was there to offer guidance...

The views expressed by the A-level students confirm that the teacher-led approach in secondary schools hinged on drill and practice and at times supported by technology, does not have a meaningful impact on the ability of students to be engaged in critical thinking. This finding further consolidates what previous research has highlighted about the development of critical thinking in students, namely that context-specific curricular tasks have significant implications for the development of critical thinking in learners (Byrne & Brodie, 2012).

During the interview, the tertiary level respondents [TEI] maintained that teaching and learning activities at the tertiary level are hardly organized around the promotion of critical thinking in the sciences. They also acknowledged that group work had not been carried out for the science subjects when they were studying at A-level and that, at times, they had organised group work on their own. Furthermore, the students stated that they had been "*completely lost*" when they had joined the tertiary institution as they had not felt adequately prepared to face the challenges at the tertiary level.

> TEI 1: ...we were facing difficulties to answer the lecturers' questions, and we were told that we were not critical enough...

During the interview, the students affirmed that they were not quite clear about what is meant by "being critical enough" during lectures and they revealed that, in some cases, they were not encouraged to have open discussions.

> TEI 1: ...there are some lecturers who do not allow questions to be asked during the lecture and, in case questions are asked, they will simply tell us that this is your homework...

They therefore resorted to working in groups to be able to pass the examinations. Furthermore, the TEI students asserted that they were not engaged in formally structured group work in the teaching-learning set-up. However, they occasionally conducted group work with selected peers during their free time. They added that they wished group work had been carried out during lectures as this would have provided them with the opportunity to think and reflect while interacting with their peers (Fry, Ketteridge, & Marshall, 2009).

> TEI 2: ...hopefully, we are able to surmount the difficulties by collaborating with our peers...

The students insisted that some lecturers still favoured strict lecturing (Hativa, 2000), which involved the dictation of notes. They also claimed that they understood that such an approach did not help them to organise their thinking for self-directed and independent learning, especially in this technology-driven era.

> TEI 2: ...we were very much surprised when we joined ...tertiary education...we were being dictated notes just as when we were in secondary school...of course, we did not like it. Also, we were viewing the PowerPoint and wasting time copying the notes from it. The lecturer could have sent us the PowerPoint by email and used lecture time for discussion...

The explanation offered by both the A-level and TEI students suggested that not enough attention was paid to the acquisition and development of soft skills by students as the focus of the teaching was principally geared towards the mastery of subject content. This promoted rote learning at the expense of critical thinking and may explain not only the relatively poor performance of the participants in the power cut problem but also the lack of clear demarcation between the performance of the TEI students and A-level students.

Though the TEI students were collaborating in groups outside the formal set-up, the evidence shows that, in general, they could to a limited extent relate their acquired knowledge and skills to a particular real-life context. Most probably because teaching and learning are still being influenced by the didactic model with a focus on examinations, thereby compromising the development of their critical thinking. Such a situation also prevails at the secondary level as indicated by the students during the interview.

5   Conclusion

The study had two research hypotheses which the use of quantitative data analysis (Friedman, Wilcoxon and Mann Whitney tests) revealed not to be true. The secondary school students performed relatively better than the tertiary level students on the 'thinking' component of critical thinking. However, no significant difference was found in the 'reflecting' and 'action' components between the two categories of students.

Additionally, it was observed that, since critical thinking involves the three components, the students did not generally perform equally-well between these components as we had conjectured. The interviews with both categories of the participants (A-level and tertiary level) enabled us to understand that critical thinking had not been a prominent element in the teaching and learning of science in secondary schools and at the TEI. The traditional teaching and examination related expectations that were dominant in secondary schools extended to the tertiary level. Unfortunately, the recent reform in the education system in the country has had little effect in bringing about the desired change. The development of 21st-century skills demands a profound transition from the didactic to the learner-centred approach, where students can display innovativeness through a reasoned course of action.

This study thus reinforces the calls for changes to be brought to curricular design, particularly for the science subjects at both secondary and tertiary levels for the promotion of 21st-century skills, such as critical thinking, among others. The power cut problem has revealed that students at both levels are not able to take prompt and judicious decisions due to their inability to make meaningful connections between knowledge acquired at school and tertiary level and real-life problems. In the long run, this shortcoming may affect our country's human resource capacity to respond to emerging crises in this technologically connected world. This may have global implications.

References

Bailin, S. (2002). Critical thinking in science education. *Science & Education, 11*, 361–375.

Barnett, R. (1997). *Higher education: A critical business.* Open University Press.

Blank, R. K., de las Alas, N., & Smith, C. (2008). *Does teacher professional development have effects on teaching and learning? Evaluation findings from programs in 14 States.* Retrieved May, 2020, from http://programs.ccsso.org/content/pdfs/cross-state_study_rpt_final.pdf

Burke, A. (2011). Group work: How to use groups effectively. *The Journal of Effective Teaching, 11*(2), 87–95.

Byrne, E., & Brodie, M. (2012). *Cross-curricular teaching & learning in the secondary school – Science.* Routledge Taylor & Francis Group.

Caracelli, V. J., & Green, J. C. (1993). Data analysis strategies for mixed-method evaluation design. *Educational Evaluation and Policy Analysis, 15*(2), 195–207.

Combs, J. P., & Onwuegbuzie, A. J. (2010). Describing and illustrating data analysis in mixed research. *International Journal of Education, 2*(2), 1–23.

Corder, G. W., & Foreman, D. I. (2009). *Nonparametric statistics for non-statisticians. A step-by-step approach.* John Wiley & Sons.

Creswell, J. P. (2012). *Educational research – Planning, conducting and evaluating quantitative and qualitative research* (4th ed.). Pearson.

Cuban, L. (2001). *Oversold and underused: Computers in the classroom.* Harvard University Press.

Davies, M. (2015). A model of critical thinking in higher education. In M. B. Paulsen (Ed.), *Higher education: Handbook of theory and research* (pp. 41–92). Springer International Publishing.

Devlin, T. J., Feldhaus, C. R., & Bentrem, K. M. (2013). The evolving classroom: A study of traditional and technology-based instruction in a STEM classroom. *Journal of Technology Education, 25*(1), 34–54.

Ennis, R. H. (2015). Critical thinking: A streamlined conception. In M. Davies & R. Barnett (Eds.), *The Palgrave handbook of critical thinking in higher education* (pp. 31–47). Palgrave Macmillan. https://doi.org/10.1057/9781137378057_2

Fields, Z. (2019). Cognitive skills development at higher educational level in the Fourth Industrial Revolution: A case for creativity. In Z. Fields, J. Bucher, & A. Weller (Eds.),

Imagination, creativity, and responsible management in the Fourth Industrial Revolution (pp. 126–157). IGI Global. doi:10.4018/978-1-5225-9188-7

Fitzgerald, M., Danaia, L., & McKinnon, D. H. (2019). Barriers inhibiting inquiry-based science teaching and potential solutions: Perceptions of positively inclined early adopters. *Research in Science Education, 49*(567), 543–566. https://doi.org/10.1007/s11165-018-9812-x

Flores, K. L., Matkin, G. S., Burbach, M. E., Quinn, C. E., & Harding, H. (2012). Deficient critical thinking skills among college graduates: Implications for leadership. *Educational Theory and Theory, 44*(2), 212–230.

Fortus, D., Krajcik, J., Dershimer, R. C., Marx, R. W., & Mamlok-Naaman, R. (2005). Design-based science and real-world problem-solving. *International Journal of Science Education, 27*(7), 855–879.

Fry, H., Ketteridge, S., & Marshall, S. (Eds.). (2009). *A handbook for teaching and learning in higher education: Enhancing academic practice.* Routledge/Taylor & Francis Group.

Giselsson, K. (2020). Critical thinking and critical literacy: Mutually exclusive? *International Journal for the Scholarship of Teaching and Learning, 14*(1), 1–9. doi:10.20429/ijsotl.2020.140105

Glaze, A. L. (2018). Teaching and learning science in the 21st century: Challenging critical assumptions in post-secondary science. *Education Sciences, 8*(12), 1–8.

Gyenes, A. (2015). Definitions of critical thinking in context. *Annals of Educational Studies, 20*, 17–25. doi:10.18910/57422

Hativa, N. (2000). Lecturing and explaining. In N. Hastiva (Ed.), *Teaching for effective learning in higher education* (pp. 71–86). Springer.

Hill, C. (2008). The post-scientific society. *Issues in Science & Technology, 24*(1), 78–84.

Hofstein, A., & Lunetta, V. N. (2003). The laboratory in science education: Foundations for the twenty-first century. *Science Education, 88*(1), 28–54.

Hume, A., & Coll, R. (2010). Authentic student inquiry: The mismatch between the intended curriculum and the student-experienced curriculum. *Research in Science & Technological Education, 28*(1), 43–62.

Isseks, M. (2011). When teachers reduce curriculum content to bullet points, student learning suffers. *Educational Leadership*, 74–76.

Jackson, S. L. (2010). *Statistics plain and simple.* Wadsworth, Cengage Printing.

Lloyd, M., & Bahr, N. (2010). Thinking critically about critical thinking in higher education. *International Journal for the Scholarship of Teaching and Learning, 4*(2), 1–17.

Müller, K., Prenzel, M., Seidel, T., Schiepe-Tiska, A., & Kjærnsli, M. (2016). Science teaching and learning in schools: Theoretical and empirical foundations for investigating classroom-level processes (pp. 424–446). In S. E. Kuger (Ed.), *Assessing contexts of learning, methodology of educational measurement and assessment.* Springer International Publishing.

Nachar, N. (2008). The Mann-Whitney U: A test for assessing whether two independent samples come from the same distribution. *Tutorials in Quantitative Methods for Psychology, 4*(1), 13–20.

NAP. (2012). *A framework for K-12 science education: Practices, crosscutting concepts and core ideas*. The National Academies Press.

National Research Council. (1996). *National science education standards*. The National Academies of Sciences, Engineering and Medicine. https://doi.org/10.17226/4962

National Research Council. (2005). *How students learn in the classroom* (S. M. Donovan & J. D. Bransford, Eds.). The National Academies Press.

Osborne, J. (2014). Teaching critical thinking? New directions in science education. *School Science Review, 95*(352), 53–62.

Ramma, Y., Bholoa, A., Watts, M., & Nadal, P. S. (2018). Teaching and learning physics using technology: Making a case for the affective domain. *Education Inquiry, 9*(2), 210–236. https://doi.org/10.1080/20004508.2017.1343606

Ramma, Y., Samy, M., & Gopee, A. (2015). Creativity and innovation in science and technology: Bridging the gap between secondary and tertiary levels of education. *International Journal of Educational Management, 29*(1), 2–17.

Rossman, G. B., & Wilson, B. L. (1994). Numbers and words revisited: Being "shamelessly eclectic". *Quality and Quantity, 28*, 315–327.

SAPEA. (2019). *Making sense of science for policy under conditions of complexity and uncertainty*. Science Advice for Policy by European Academies. Retrieved May, 2020, from https://www.sapea.info/topics/making-sense-of-science/

Scott, L. C. (2015). *The futures of learning 2: What kind of learning for the 21st century?* UNESCO Education Research and Foresight.

Sointu, E., Hirsto, L., & Murtonen, M. (2019). Transforming higher education teaching and learning environments – Introduction to the special issue. *International Journal of Learning, Teaching and Educational Research, 18*(13), 1–6.

Stein, B., Haynes, A., Redding, M., Ennis, T., & Cecil, M. (2007). Assessing critical thinking in STEM and beyond. In M. Iskander (Ed.), *Innovation in e-learning, instruction technology, assessment and engineering education* (pp. 79–82). Springer.

Teddlie, C., Tashakkori, A., & Johnson, R. B. (2008). Emergent techniques in the gathering and analysis of mixed methods data. In S. N. Hesse-Biber & P. Leavy (Eds.), *Handbook of emergent methods* (pp. 389–414). The Guilford Press.

Timothy, D. J., Feldhaus, C. R., & Bentrem, K. M. (2013). The evolving classroom: A study of traditional and technology-based instruction in a STEM classroom. *Journal of Technology Education, 25*(1), 34–54.

Tondeur, J., van Braak, J., Sang, G., Vougt, J., Fisser, P., & Ottenbreit-Leftwich, A. (2012). Preparing pre-service teachers to integrate technology in education: A synthesis of qualitative evidence. *Computers & Education, 59*, 134–144.

Waysman, M., & Savaya, R. (1997). Mixed method evaluation: A case study. *Evaluation Practice, 18*(3), 227–237.

WEF. (2015). *New vision for education: Unlocking the potential of technology.* Retrieved April 2020, from http://www3.weforum.org/docs/WEFUSA_NewVisionforEducation_Report2015.pdf

CHAPTER 10

Genius-Hour: Student-Led Learning in the Fourth Industrial Revolution

Jennifer M. Schneider and Guy Trainin

Abstract

This chapter looks at the implementation of inquiry-based learning in Genius-Hour, a K-12 classroom learning strategy. For this project, Jerome Bruner's constructivist learning theory research and the link to motivation in the classroom as theorized by Daniel Pink and Peter Gray's study of structured play were combined to establish a concrete foundation. With a focus on building a constructivist culture through Dewey's experiential Learning by Doing, Genius-Hour originated as a learning design. Fostering inquiry, creativity, research, and collaboration through exploring learner-generated essential questions, Genius-Hour expands project-based/problem-based learning to passion-based learning. The key research question for this study is, *What are students' perceptions of participating in Genius Hour in the classroom*? Two participants were interviewed about their experience in the project. The themes we identified in the interviews included independence, support, motivation, and mentorship. Artifacts from successful Genius-Hour projects and qualitative data based on learning experiences are included in the chapter. This project outlined in this chapter follows learner perceptions and the implications to and a district's investment to implement a school-wide program for all students regardless of achievement on state and national standards. Using this unique approach to learning and technologies, teachers and students will become 21st-century learners as they embrace the Fourth Industrial Revolution.

1 Introduction

Inquiry-based learning projects, in the form of Genius-Hour and other discovery-oriented learning projects, are growing in popularity in K-12 classrooms, which include students from ages 5 through 18. Genius-Hour is drawn from Google's 20% time in which Google employees can spend 20% of their workweek, working on their own projects and Daniel Pink's 2009 TED Talk, "The Puzzle of Motivation", which talks about "autonomy, mastery, and purpose" and how the Google model reflects these concepts. In his book, Pink encouraged the use of 20% time in the classroom in similar ways to address the factors that cause motivation to go down as students get older (Pink, 2011).

After watching Pink's TED Talk, I (the first author) started to think about implementing Genius-Hour in my own classroom. As a middle school Language Arts teacher, much of my time was being spent preparing students for state assessments. In 2014, I was in my ninth year in the classroom and frustrated by the disconnect between what I was teaching and what students were passionate about or wanted to explore. My students echoed this frustration. I had already started implementing inquiry projects where students were researching a topic, giving a speech, and teaching their classmates about a specific topic. However, my students and I wanted more. Genius-Hour provided an avenue to deeper inquiry, connection to community and career interests, and engagement.

Inquiry-based learning, or IBL, is defined as an approach that uses questioning to stimulate students and aim to construct new knowledge in pursuit of answering that question (Spronken-Smith et al., 2008). IBL is often used as an umbrella term that is used for different levels of inductive methods, but there are distinctions within inductive teaching methods. Typically, these methods are taught by supplying the students with a problem or a question to solve. These methods are distinguished by the teaching approach. *Inquiry-based learning* begins with a problem or challenge in which prior knowledge is not necessarily applicable and curricular knowledge has not yet occurred. This question or challenge may be presented by the instructor, and the students attempt to solve the problem with their own research (Prince & Felder, 2007). Quite often, student research is guided by the instructor as a facilitator. The foundation of inquiry-based learning is questions driven by real-life observations. *Problem-based learning* (PBL), in contrast, addresses ill-structured problems for students to solve through varied analysis and research (Oguz-Ünver & Arabacıoğlu, 2011). PBL often assumes that students come with background knowledge or curriculum focused on helping them solve the given problem. Still another distinction in these inductive methods is *project-based learning*, which calls for the student to address a question or challenge but produce something as a result (performance, paper, artifact) (Prince & Felder, 2007). Inquiry-based research is more prominent than problem-based research at the K-12 level (Oguz-Ünver & Arabacıoğlu, 2011). Genius-Hour (also known as passion projects or 20 percent time) is a culmination of these methods, drawing from the questioning approach of inquiry-based learning, the student-guided approach of problem-based learning, and the final product of project-based learning.

Spronken-Smith and her colleagues (2012) studied cases of higher education inquiry-based learning courses, including student perceptions of the learning process and intended outcomes. The study used a quantitative survey measure for data collection to measure students' perceptions of their participation in IBL courses based on the mode (structured, guided, or open) and framing (information or discovery-oriented). Findings were that students that experienced more open discovery-oriented approaches (similar to Genius-Hour) had more positive perceptions of learning outcomes.

The gap in the literature regarding student perceptions of inquiry-based learning methods is in the lack of research on student perceptions at the middle school level for open, discovery-oriented teaching and learning methods.

2   What Is Genius-Hour?

Before starting Genius-Hour, I asked my students what bothered them about school. Several students responded regarding the relevance of what they were learning and how it applied to real life. One student reported, "It bothers me that I am not learning things in school that will help me with what I want to do when I grow up". Although middle school students may not be fully aware of their long-term life goals, the notion of relevance is critical for 21st-century students as we enter the Fourth Industrial Revolution – what people do must matter. Education in the Fourth Industrial Revolution must develop students who know how to independently pursue their interests and goals.

Constructivist learning approaches allow students to gain knowledge and apply it to their own experiences and the world around them. Traditional schooling often focuses on the specific and concrete while Genius Hour brings in the abstract, applicable knowledge beyond the curriculum. "In the case of the so-called disciplinary or pre-eminently logical studies, there is danger of the isolation of intellectual activity from the ordinary affairs of lie" (Dewey, 1916). Dewey's early approach to learning is seen through Genius Hour and other PBL methods.

During Genius-Hour, knowledge work is ongoing and adaptable. Students use their unique perspectives, and learning is individualized as students focus on their learning goals and potential careers. This mode of learning moves teachers away from the front of the class as conveyors of knowledge to serve as facilitators and coaches (Karagiorgi & Symeou, 2005). While it fits the Fourth Industrial Revolution, this approach harkens back to the principles of Dewey (1916), Bruner (1961) and Korczak (1942), focusing on student-centered learning.

Genius-Hour starts with respect to the individual learner, regardless of age or development, coming up with an essential question that extends beyond a Google search. Topics in Genius-Hour are open-ended, which allows students to explore myriad interests. Questions ranging from "How do I create an app that helps me remember science vocabulary?" to "How can we provide clean water to developing countries?" bring students into the world and embrace the Fourth Industrial Revolution (Schwab, 2016). Students then use a collaborative design process to arrive at a product that serves as an interrogative answer to the essential question. Teachers serve as coaches who provide research assistance through teaching digital literacy and inquiry skills. Electronic communication allows students to collaborate outside the classroom and reach mentors with specialized knowledge applicable to their essential questions. This technology, so central to the Fourth Industrial Revolution, affords students an extended learning community. Ultimately, the product is shared with the learning community and even beyond. The question guiding this study was to examine the feasibility and impact of Genius-hour in the middle school curriculum.

3 Methodology

3.1 *Sample Selection*

We used purposive sampling to maximize the depth of potential impact with two students who were engaged with Genius-Hour during their last year of middle school and were willing, four years later, to examine the impact Genius-Hour had on their lives and learning. Students were selected from my classroom (first author) in a suburban middle school close to Title 1 status (almost 40% free and reduced lunch).

Katie was an eighth-grade at-risk student who was living with her parents, niece, and five siblings. She is one of 12 children in her family. Katie's eighth-grade Genius-Hour project involved art. At the start of the project, Katie had no experience with art creation or technique. Her extracurricular activities prior to the project included track and field and cross country running. By the time we wrote up this study Katie was working part-time: caring for her grandmother, raising a child, and planning on attending art school the following year.

Tamara lived at home with her mother, father, and sister. Tamara created clothing from patterns and was interested in fashion design prior to starting the project. During her Genius-Hour experience, she obtained an in-person mentor, a then 19-year-old emerging fashion designer. By the time we wrote up the study Tamara had gained basic experience in sewing and creating fashion designs without patterns. Tamara is now a first-generation college student studying construction management while designing her own clothing and attending fashion shows and events. In February 2020, she was one of 40 women selected from the United States and Canada to attend Kiewit Corporation's Women in Engineering and Construction Leadership seminar.

3.2 *Participant Perspectives*

In this study, the focus is on the student participants' perceptions of their experiences in the inquiry-based learning project. Themes reflected multiple perspectives from the different participants. The study's themes emerged from the data, as we tried to preserve student words and intent as much as possible.

3.3 *Methods*

The purpose of this instrumental case study was to explore middle school general education students' perceptions of participation in an inquiry-based learning project: Genius-Hour. Findings related to student perceptions, motivations, and challenges were examined to suggest ways to better deliver Genius-Hour. The project sought to address the problem of relevance and applicability to learning and career goals as students experience innovative inquiry-driven education.

The research on inquiry-based learning is extensive, but little has been studied regarding student perceptions of participating in Genius-Hour or similar inquiry-based projects across the curriculum. Much of the research regarding the impact of inquiry-based learning has been quantitative in nature.

The philosophical assumptions which characterize qualitative research make a qualitative design preferable over a quantitative approach for this study. Considering the epistemological assumption, qualitative researchers attempt to gain understanding through the subjective experiences of the participants. Qualitative research typically begins with the interest of the researcher that leads to a problem that addresses a particular need for ongoing research (Babchuk & Badiee, 2010). Genius-Hour and inquiry-based learning were our primary research interests, and we have been pursuing ways to (a) help students gain more access to experts in their individual fields of interest and (b) use instructional technology to increase student motivation and acquisition of knowledge within their inquiry-based learning and Genius-Hour studies.

Data were obtained in the natural setting of the study, the classroom and through observations and interviews, making qualitative research (case study) the optimal design for this study. Qualitative research uses face-to-face interaction over a given period of time (Creswell, 2015), which is a factor that will be pertinent to this study. The study was completed using interviews and artifacts from two post-secondary students that participated in Genius-Hour while in middle school.

3.4 *Data Collection Method*

To begin the Genius-Hour projects, students first filled out a brainstorming form to help them decide what their interests are and what they would like to study. Next, students completed a question generation form to determine questions they may ask concerning the topics they are interested in. Finally, students completed a Genius-Hour proposal form and a video "elevator pitch" that was approved by their classroom teacher. Proposals were denied only if logistical, financial, or safety concerns were factors. Informed consent did not need to be obtained for all students completing these forms as they are part of the Genius-Hour curriculum.

During this study, interviews and artifacts were used. Data was collected through semi-structured interviews, using open-ended questions. One interview was completed via email because of scheduling difficulties with the participant. The other interview was completed in person.

3.5   *Documents & Artifacts*

Initial data (prior to sample selection) was obtained via Genius-Hour brainstorming forms, question generation forms, and Genius-Hour proposal forms. Student project artifacts (i.e. research notes, blogs, physical projects) were also used in data collection.

3.6   *Interviews*

Individual interviews were conducted in person (when possible) with participants. Since students may be influenced by their peers' answers or reluctant to speak honestly when other students are present, this method produced more valid results. The interviews were semi-structured, guided by a list of open-ended flexibly worded questions with follow-up questions emerging from participants' answers (Merriam & Tisdell, 2016).

In order to gain a deeper understanding of the phenomenon during the data collection process, semi-structured interview questions are used. Questions were carefully worded in language that is understandable and relevant to participants. By carefully choosing words (sans jargon or difficult vocabulary), participants were more likely to provide relevant, sensible answers (Patton, 2015). To obtain basic information about the participant, Patton's six types of questions were used: experience and behavior questions (to explore experiences with their project and utilizing a digital mentor), opinions and values questions (to measure perceptions of motivation), feeling questions (to measure perceptions/feelings closely related to the experience and behavior questions), knowledge questions (to assess projects and information related to the content), sensory questions (to elicit more data related to experience and behavior but in context of what is being seen, heard, or felt), and limited background/demographic questions (Merriam & Tisdell, 2016). Probes such as "tell me more" or "what does _____ mean?" may be used to clarify responses or allow participants to elaborate (Creswell, 2015, p. 220).

4 Theoretical Framework

Dewey's theory of Learning by Doing and Experiential Learning framed this study. Dewey explored the idea of interest in education. According to Dewey (1916), interest is any experience having a purpose. When students reported their concerns of being disconnected from their learning, their lack of purpose in education was exemplified. In addition, Dewey's model of learning finds that learning occurs when students have a desire to learn (Kolb, 1984).

Within the study, we explored the role of the teacher or the mentor in influencing students' perceptions of participating in Genius-Hour in the classroom. Children are greatly influenced by teachers' habits and presentation of particular subject matter (Dewey, 1910). With project-based learning, teachers serve as facilitators of learning rather than lecturers. During the study, we analyzed the perceptions of the participants before and after having teacher or mentor direction.

The experience will not result in meaningful learning without some independent thinking or reflection (Dewey, 1916), which is why this study also explores students' perceptions of their Genius-Hour experience including their initial knowledge acquisition without the direction of a mentor.

5 Findings, Analysis and Discussion

5.1 *Analytic Procedure*
After the interviews, I read through all data, adding margin notes, and forming initial codes. Drawing from these codes, themes were generalized, and a detailed description of the case and its setting was generated from the data (Creswell, 2013). Categorical aggregation (Stake, 1995) was used in order to determine relevant meanings and themes that emerged from the collected data from individual interviews and artifacts. Data was reviewed multiple times to generalize themes (Creswell, 2013).

Looking at the codes and themes, I interpreted the larger meaning of the data in connection and context of the larger body of research literature pertaining to the themes in the study. In the study, validity was ensured by using multiple methods (interviews and artifacts). Validity in the formal study should be increased by using triangulation through obtaining data via multiple methods of data collection including interviews, observations, and documents and artifacts. By looking at the codes and generalized themes from the multiple methods, these findings can be deemed valid.

From the codes and categories, we identified emergent themes regarding the perceptions of working with digital mentors. During this iteration of the study, pre-interview questions were given, so the analysis is highly interpretative (Stake, 1995), and additional themes may emerge with observation, added participants, and during the project and post-project interviews.

5.2 Independence before Mentorship

The first theme that emerged in the study was the need for independence before mentorship. Since in Genius-Hour essential questions are not focused on current skill levels or prior knowledge, both Katie and Tamara had limited knowledge about their topic. Katie said that she did not have much knowledge about art and focused on the fun. This meant that Katie had to find her own passion and style before getting connected with a mentor in high school the following year. This theme emerged in the context of beginning knowledge and need for exploration through the interviews.

> **Katie:** I was just getting into art, so I feel like I had to find myself and find where I was going. I just kind of did it. I wanted to work with paint, and it gave me an opportunity to.

Tamara had a basic knowledge of sewing and working from patterns but emphasized that she had never experienced this type of learning before. Both students were able to work independently before finding a mentor through class or on their own after the course had ended. Katie said that it was important to work on her own first.

> **Tamara:** I had never done anything like this before.
> **Katie:** I had to find myself and find where I was going. I wanted to put my skills to the test and see what I could really achieve on my own.

The transcripts above showed the fundamental need for exploration and independence before mentorship through teachers or community members were introduced. Since knowledge is an adaptive process, students can construct knowledge regardless of teacher input (Karagiorgi & Symeou, 2005). By its very nature, inquiry-based learning and problem-based learning methods like Genius-Hour are student-centered. Knowledge is constructed by the student, often with minimal background knowledge research (Oguz-Ünver & Arabacıoğlu, 2011).

In coursework outside of Genius-Hour, often teachers give students questions to answer. Students then focus on the answer that will be most pleasing to the teacher rather than their own knowledge acquisition. This is particularly true when students have a positive relationship with the teacher (Dewey, 1910). It was

GENIUS-HOUR 165

important for the students to experience their own research and exploration separate from teacher or mentor influence during the infancy of their projects.

As knowledge is the combination of individual life experiences and objective social experiences as learned through traditional schooling (Kolb, 1984), the students' Genius-Hour experiences were shaped by the knowledge obtained by research and asking questions as well as their own personal desires to explore their art on their own.

The impact of knowledge acquisition and independence on student perceptions of Genius-Hour is evident through the interviews and Katie's initial painting (Figure 10.1). Katie explored different painting techniques on her own. She did not have an art mentor to guide her during her Genius-Hour project. Her unique style (Figure 10.2) emerged after working with an art mentor and collaborators in high school.

FIGURE 10.1   Katie's To Kill a Mockingbird ceiling tile

5.3   *Collaborators and Supports*

The second theme that emerged was the need for collaborators and supports in achieving goals. Although Katie and Tamara did not have mentors at the onset of their projects, both mentioned people who pushed them or encouraged them to reach their goals. This theme of the need for collaborators and support was found through the interview data in connection with the study of experiential learning.

> **Katie:** I met a few artists in this group called Pipe Dreams like young artists in the metro area that get together and do art together…I have this really cool art teacher now…she is an amazing person. She really pushes

FIGURE 10.2
Katie's work in 2019

me hard to keep on making art...I have a lot of friends that will help me out and give me pointers on things when it comes to art like drawing.

As their projects progressed, Katie found collaborators (i.e. other artists) to be important in helping her perfect her craft. In addition, Katie was able to find a mentor in high school through her art teacher. This was after she had explored her style in middle school. Her mentor, however, was pivotal in helping her make connections in the art community and develop her own style.

Tamara worked with a 19-year-old mentor who was emerging as a designer in the area. During Tamara's Genius Hour project time, her mentor presented her clothing line at New York full-figured fashion week. In addition, Tamara and her mentor attended local fashion shows and a business/entrepreneur conference for students. These experiences helped Tamara find her own style while having someone to cheer her on and help her succeed.

Tamara: ...was a huge encouragement to know that someone was... cheering for me to be successful.

Tamara's experience with her mentor also helped her develop leadership skills that lead to her current education path in construction management.

She is also a student officer for her college's Associated General Contractors of America club.

The relationship between the teacher and student and the subject matter itself shapes students' perceptions in any educational subject. The role of an educator is not to guarantee student interest but "furnish the environment which stimulates responses and directs the learner's course" (Dewey, 1916, p. 212). During Katie's project, the teacher provided the tools and the environment to ask questions and let work become play. In this case, providing that environment set Katie up to explore independently and eventually find her own mentor in high school and a group of collaborators.

As for Tamara, the role of her experienced mentor after shaped her perceptions of Genius-Hour. The role of the mentor mirrors Dewey's interpretation of the instructor role. The interview transcript indicates that her mentor introduced the standards of design and recognized the possibilities that Tamara had to make her own creations. In fact, the teacher or mentor role should be focused on the students' needs and capabilities rather than the subject matter at hand (Dewey, 1916). This was the case with Tamara as her mentor met with her to help her reach her goals in her own original design by providing guidance tailored to the student.

The artifact in Figure 10.3 is indicative of the influence of Tamara's mentor on supporting her design capabilities.

FIGURE 10.3
Tamara's "Scout" dress on a model

5.4 *Student Motivation*

Student motivation and the connection to learner development was a third theme that came forth through the study. For both students, Genius Hour was a project that was fueled by a desire to learn something relevant to their own interests, regardless of prior knowledge. This theme came forward through the interviews conducted with the student participants.

Katie did not know a lot about art going into the project but was motivated by enjoyment and engagement in the classroom.

> **Katie:** ...usually that's the first thing I wanted to do because I was into it and really liked it and it was fun.

Katie's motivation to complete her artwork during Genius Hour showed how she developed as an artist and a learner still today.

> **Katie:** It was something to fill my time, and it was fun. I do that a lot with projects nowadays too. I like start it and I finish it, and that's all I want to do.

Before the project began, Tamara had some foundation level knowledge when it came to sewing and design.

> **Tamara:** I knew how to sew and had already created a couple of pieces of garments, but I wanted to expand my knowledge in the fashion world and create more challenging pieces of clothing.

Through learning additional skills and engaging in her weekly Genius-Hour time, Tamara was able to develop as a designer, entrepreneur, and a learner.

> **Tamara:** A successful Genius-Hour project would challenge a person's abilities but also allow them to learn about a subject that they had much interest in and may not have known or had much experience with before.

This challenge motivated Tamara as a learner as is evident in the excerpt that follows.

> **Tamara:** I was very motivated to complete this project. I had never done anything like this before and how to come up with a way to show who this character was a two-garment piece.

When students are able to engage their "natural impulses" and play, school is a positive experience and motivation to learn and work increases (Dewey, 1916, p. 229). Children, by nature, have a natural instinct to play (Gray, 2013). While traditional schooling often requires work before play, Genius-Hour offers the opportunity to link work to play. Even though the work was challenging, the ability to explore and experience learning without constraints motivated both students to finish their projects.

Activities that involve play and hands-on work, as in these Genius-Hour projects, are motivating because of their usefulness outside the classroom (Dewey, 1916). The key principles of motivation: autonomy, mastery, and purpose are reflected in our participants' perceptions of Genius-Hour (Pink, 2011). First, both students had an autonomous desire to find their own direction and style before working with a mentor. In addition, Tamara stated that she wanted to improve her skills and expand her knowledge. This motivation pointed to mastery as a key principle in motivation and the desire to improve her skill set. Finally, both students found a greater purpose through their projects. Their perceptions of Genius-Hour through the interviews and future experiences show that they have continued pursuits in art (Katie) and business (Tamara).

6 Conclusion

Findings from this study can be used to design the next iteration of Genius-Hour in the secondary classroom to support 21st-century learning. The findings from this initial study answer the question, "*What are students' perceptions of participating in Genius Hour in the classroom?*" and show that for some students the experiences during Genius-hour can be life-altering, initiating careers and opening avenues for personal growth. Since the study was completed with two students who had already participated in a year-long implementation of Genius-Hour, their success stories and growth are an example of education for the Fourth Industrial Revolution. The students used their own initiative and interest to create a new path, in doing that they learned how to harness their own motivation to learn and develop. Both students started the project with little to no knowledge of their topics of interest. Now, both are continuing to pursue their initial inquiries. Katie refers to art as her "career" now. Tamara chose a path outside of fashion but found opportunities and connections during the project that led her to an entrepreneurial field in construction management. Within the study, the students interviewed wanted to find their own interests and work on their own before being introduced to a mentor. This theme, need for independence before mentorship highlights the need for initial time for exploration and play before formal instruction in a trade or career field.

The themes emerging from the study included: the need for independence before mentorship, need for collaborators and support, and student motivation and the connection to learner development. Next steps in the study include finding additional avenues to reach out to community mentors for students in different interest areas. After exploring their own passions through independent learning and research, students will be connected with mentors to strengthen the Genius-Hour experience. The authors have explored avenues through LinkedIn groups, community partnerships, and social media connections. These avenues will be implemented in the next iteration of the study.

Participants utilized technology to pursue their interests further, even before formal mentorship. Teachers can use Genius-Hour in the 21st-century to help their students embrace the Fourth Industrial Revolution. Studying topics relevant to career interests or simply exploring ideas that enhance learning will help students transition into a new digital age of collaboration, student-centered acquisition of knowledge, and asynchronous learning that extends outside the classroom walls.

We suggest that further instrumental case studies as well as design studies regarding the impacts of Genius-Hour with in-person mentors may be conducted and used to support expanding these practices.

References

Babchuk, W. A., & Badiee, M. (2010, September 26–28). *Realizing the potential of qualitative designs: A conceptual guide for research and practice*. Paper presented at Midwest Research-to-Practice Conference in Adult, Continuing, and Community Education.

Creswell, J. W. (2013). *Qualitative inquiry and research design: Choosing among five approaches*. Sage.

Creswell, J. W. (2016). *30 Essential skills for the qualitative researcher*. Sage.

Dewey, J. (1910). *How we think: A restatement of the relation of reflective thinking to the educative process*. D.C. Heath and Company.

Dewey, J. (1916). *Democracy and education: An introduction to the philosophy of education*. Macmillan.

Gray, P. (2013). *Free to learn: Why unleashing the instinct to play will make our children happier, more self-reliant, and better students for life*. Basic Books.

Karagiorgi, Y., & Symeou, L. (2005). Translating constructivism into instructional design: Potential and limitations. *Educational Technology & Society, 8*(1), 17–27.

Kolb, D. A. (1984). *Experiential learning: Experience as the source of learning and development*. Prentice-Hall.

Merriam, S. B., & Tisdell, E. J. (2016). *Qualitative research: A guide to design and implementation*. Jossey-Bass.

Oguz-Ünver, A., & Arabacioglu, S. (2011). Overviews on inquiry-based and problem based learning methods. *Western Anatolia Journal of Educational Science*, 303–309.

Pajares, F., & Graham, L. (1999). Self-efficacy, motivation constructs, and mathematics performance of entering middle school students. *Contemporary Educational Psychology, 24*(2), 124–139.

Patton, M. Q. (2015). *Qualitative research and evaluation methods* (4th ed.). Sage.

Pink, D. (2009). The puzzle of motivation [Video]. Ted.com. http://www.ted.com/talks/dan_pink_on_motivation?language=en

Pink, D. (2011). *Drive: The surprising truth about what motivates us*. Riverhead Books.

Prince, M., & Felder, R. (2007). The many faces of inductive teaching and learning. *Journal of College Science Teaching, 36*(5), 14–20.

Spronken-Smith, R., Walker, R., Batchelor, J., O'Steen, B., & Angelo, T. (2012). Evaluating student perceptions of learning processes and intended learning outcomes under inquiry approaches. *Assessment & Evaluation in Higher Education, 37*(1), 57–72.

Stake, R. (1995). *The art of case study research*. Sage.

Yin, R. K. (2003). *Case study research: Design and method* (3rd ed.). Sage.

Glossary

21st-century classroom The 21st-century classroom is student-centered, where teachers are the facilitators of learning. The learning milieu incorporates the use of technology-based tools.

21st-century skills skills, abilities, and learning dispositions that have been identified as being required for success in 21st-century society and workplaces by educators, business leaders, academics, and governmental agencies. The four skills, namely, communication, collaboration, critical thinking, and creativity, are essential inside the 21st-century classroom.

21st-century teacher a person who facilitates the teaching and learning process to enable students to become useful to themselves and society. He/she is the one who makes classroom interactive through the use of ICT and other technologies.

Affordances the possibilities that a technological tool offers to a user to make sense of a concept or to make inferences.

Algorithm a step-by-step procedure or sequence of instructions for solving a problem.

Apps applications that are available via the e-store for download on smart devices and tablets.

Artificial Intelligence (AI) when robots/machine can mimic human behavior.

Automation automatically controlled operations.

Big data very large structured and unstructured data sets that are analyzed using computers to reveal trends.

Blended learning a method of learning in which students learn through the use of technology-based tools and the traditional teaching methods, for example, 'chalk and talk'.

Bring Your Own Device (BYOD) a concept where people are allowed to bring and use their own portable devices such as smartphones, laptops, tablets, etc. to work/institution and access the network instead of the work/ institution supplying a device.

Case study activities short, structured tasks, linked to real-life examples of technological challenges in the society or community. They allow for the application of theory to solve a practical problem.

Coding the programming of algorithms using a computer language.

Computational thinking involves problem-solving skills encompassing screen-based coding, digital tangibles and off-screen algorithms.

Computer Algebra Systems (CAS) a mathematical software that can manipulate algebraic expressions and equations.

Crackers a person who identifies defects in security systems with the intent of malicious harm.

Cyberbullying an electronic form of bullying or harassment. Such bullying takes place online, and teenagers are common victims of such crime.

Deep learning a subsection of machine learning that is associated with AI. Deep learning is also known as a deep neural network, consists of networks that are capable of learning unsupervised and unstructured data.

Differentiated instruction a philosophy of teaching which considers and accommodates students' diversity in terms of their readiness to learn.

Digital learning a style of learning that is complemented by technology or by a pedagogy that makes use of technology-based tools. It incorporates different types of learning, including: blended and flipped learning.

Digital tools tools that are characterized by electronic or computerized technologies, for example, cell phones, computers, laptops, iPads and so on.

E-learning generally platforms or environment that are created online enabling distance education.

Embedded systems a computer system with a dedicated function.

Fourth Industrial Revolution usually called Industry 4.0 or 4IR, is the current and developmental transformation in the ways human function, which is as a result of technologies and trends such as, the Internet of Things (IoT), virtual reality robotics and Artificial Intelligence(AI). The Fourth Industrial Revolution characterizes new ways in which technology becomes embedded within our society and our bodies.

Genius-hour a specific inquiry-based learning project in which students have approximately one hour a week (minimum) to research, create a product, and share their research. The timeline for Genius-Hour is infinite. Students may continue to work on their Genius-Hour project after leaving the course.

Graphical User Interface (GUI) visual components on software such as labels, buttons, drop-down menus, etc.

Hackers a person who identifies defects in security systems and works to improve the system.

Identity theft the impersonation of a person online and provides credible information about that person.

Inquiry-based learning project project in which the student chooses an effective question to guide their own research, design, and presentation. Teachers act as instructional guides.

Internet of things (IoT) a networked world of connected devices, objects, and people that are aligned to the needs of individuals and society as it was created to make life easy, and information more accessible. The IoT refers to the trend whereby all sorts of objects and devices are increasingly being connected to one another via the Internet.

Internet troll an individual who distracts people by starting arguments, quarrels and upsets people on the Internet.

Machine Learning (ML) learning about statistical models and algorithms that computer systems use to achieve a precise task. This type of learning does not require explicit instructions but relies on patterns and inferences. It is considered a part of Artificial Intelligence.

m-learning a form of education and training delivered and conducted via the Internet using mobile devices, such as tablets and smartphones. It is designed to be flexible, allowing access to education anywhere, anytime.

Post-Digital Age the Digital Age or Information Age started around the 1970s with the introduction of the personal computer. Before this was the pre-Digital Age and in the midst was the mid-Digital Age. Therefore the post-Digital Age would include the current period we live in.

RAM the primary memory that stores data temporarily.

Sensor a device that provides information about the state of the robot and its environment.

Simulation mathematical techniques for imitating the behavior of situations.

Visual manipulative images, objects or other symbolic artefacts that can be manipulated either physically or mentally.

Visual mediators images, objects or other symbolic artefacts that stimulate the mind into thinking concretely about a specific concept or idea.

Visual-analytic thinking analytical reasoning supported by interactive visual images, objects and artefacts.

Index

21st-century classroom VII–IX, 5, 72–74, 77, 78, 82, 83, 92
21st-century curriculum VII, VIII, 4
21st-century skills IX, 7, 8, 72, 90–92, 94–96, 98, 99, 107, 112, 117, 140, 152
21st-century student 7, 8, 74, 159
21st-century teacher IX, 4, 6, 8, 89, 91–93, 96, 98, 100

applications (Apps) X, 4, 17, 19, 26, 36, 37, 44, 45, 60, 75
Artificial Intelligence (AI) 2, 15, 17, 19, 31, 41, 45, 107
automation 16, 24, 173

blended learning 5, 73, 82, 173

coding VIII, 18, 24, 30–33, 39, 42, 44, 45, 77, 83, 110, 111, 126
computational thinking 15, 18, 24, 39, 40, 42, 44
Computer Algebra Systems (CAS) 14, 173
cyberbullying 35, 39, 45

digital learning 15, 72
digital tools 72–74, 80

educational technology 32, 139
e-learning 44, 45, 122, 174
embedded systems 174

Fourth Industrial Revolution VII–IX, 1, 2, 6–8, 13, 15, 19, 22, 30, 31, 44, 45, 53, 55, 71–74, 76–78, 83, 89, 90, 101, 106, 117, 119–121, 140, 157, 159, 160, 169, 170, 174

Internet of Things (IoT) IX, 2, 15, 16, 19, 21, 24, 26, 31, 32, 34, 107, 108, 110–117, 174

learning VII–XI, 1–8, 14–26, 31–37, 39, 41, 44–46, 54, 55, 57, 61, 63, 65–66, 71–75, 78–83, 90–101, 106–117, 119–132, 139–142, 149, 150–152, 157–161, 163–165, 167–170

mathematics VIII–X, 13–26, 34, 35, 40, 42, 54–56, 58, 68, 71, 75, 82, 119–121, 125–127, 132, 140
m-learning 121, 122, 175

pre-service teachers 2, 106, 116, 119–121, 123, 125

science X, 6, 25, 39, 40, 42, 59, 60, 61, 68, 107, 139–144, 149, 150, 152, 160
Science, Mathematics, Engineering and Technology (STEM) 16, 17, 22, 25, 35, 40,
simulation 19, 24, 41, 60, 62, 108, 175
student VII–XI, 2–8, 14, 16–19, 21–25, 30–39, 41–45, 65, 72–75, 79–83, 90–101, 107–110, 113–115, 120–122, 127–132, 140–145, 147–152, 157–170
student-centered teaching 89, 94

teacher VII–XI, 2–8, 14, 15, 18–21, 26, 31–35, 37, 41, 42, 44–46, 54–57, 66, 71–75, 77–80, 82, 83, 89–101, 106–108, 110, 111, 114–117, 119–133, 140–142, 149, 150, 158–160, 162–167, 170
teaching VII–XI, 1–8, 14, 17–24, 31, 32, 34, 53–55, 61, 66, 72–74, 76, 78–82, 90–99, 101, 106–111, 113, 115–117, 119–123, 125–132, 139–142, 149, 150–152, 158–160
technological pedagogical content knowledge (TPACK) 95, 96, 123–125, 130, 132, 133
technology VII, IX, X, 2–7, 14, 16–18, 21, 22, 26, 32, 35–36, 39, 41, 42, 44, 45, 54–57, 60, 63, 67, 68, 71–83, 90–92, 95, 96, 101, 106–108, 110, 117, 119–124, 125–127, 130–132, 139, 140, 149–151, 160, 161, 170
technology education IX, 3, 36, 62, 108, 110, 119, 120, 121, 125–127, 131, 132

visualization IX, 17–19, 53, 56, 57, 59–61, 63–68, 107

Printed in the United States
by Baker & Taylor Publisher Services